The Sword and the Sage: Unveiling the Truth of Excalibur and Merlin

Myrddin Sage

Published by Myrddin Sage, 2024.

While every precaution has been taken in the preparation of this book, the publisher assumes no responsibility for errors or omissions, or for damages resulting from the use of the information contained herein.

THE SWORD AND THE SAGE: UNVEILING THE TRUTH OF EXCALIBUR AND MERLIN

First edition. July 6, 2024.

Copyright © 2024 Myrddin Sage.

ISBN: 979-8227072467

Written by Myrddin Sage.

Table of Contents

The Sword and the Sage: Unveiling the Truth of Excalibur and Merlin

Master the Legends and Discover the Historical Facts in Weeks – No More Myths, Only Truths

Preface

"The great enemy of the truth is very often not the lie—deliberate, contrived, and dishonest—but the myth—persistent, persuasive, and unrealistic." - John F. Kennedy.**

Few tales are as enduring or enigmatic in the tapestry of history and legend as those of Excalibur and Merlin. These stories have captivated the imagination for centuries, weaving into the fabric of cultural identity and historical inquiry. Yet, beneath their captivating narratives lies a labyrinth of myth and misconception that often obscures the truth. This book seeks to dispel these myths by delving into the factual historical context behind the legends of Excalibur and Merlin, providing a clear delineation between romanticized tales and historical truths.

As an author deeply fascinated by the rich tapestry of Arthurian legends, I became increasingly frustrated by the scarcity of resources that comprehensively addressed the mythological and historical aspects. This frustration was echoed in conversations with fellow enthusiasts who craved a more profound understanding but were met with fragmented narratives. Inspired by this shared thirst for knowledge, I embarked on a journey to create a guide that not only entertains but educates—offering clarity and insight into these beloved stories.

Imagine a reader like Alice, who grew up enchanted by the tales of knights and wizards but, as an adult historian, seeks to understand the true essence behind these stories. Or consider Bob, a medieval reenactor who strives to portray his characters as accurately as possible but needs help with conflicting sources. Their frustrations mirror those experienced by many who find themselves lost between lore and reality. It was for Alice, Bob, and countless others that I felt compelled to write this book.

Throughout this journey, I have been fortunate to draw inspiration from various sources. Historical texts provided a foundation, while literary critiques offered modern interpretations that guided my narrative approach. I am particularly grateful to scholars whose extensive research into Celtic history helped shape the chapters on Merlin's origins.

To all who embark on reading this book, thank you for investing your time in uncovering the truths behind these legendary figures. Whether you are a student of history, a lover of mythology, or someone intrigued by Arthurian tales, I hope this book connects you to the rich historical truths that ground these enchanting legends.

This book is intended for anyone who seeks a factual understanding of Arthurian legend's captivating tales. Other prerequisites are curiosity and a willingness to explore myth and history with an open mind.

Thank you for choosing to delve deeper into this subject with me. I invite you to continue reading and join me in unveiling the rich truths hidden within these legendary narratives. Together, let us explore the myths and the profound realities they conceal.

Chapter 1: The Metamorphosis of Excalibur

The morning air was crisp, carrying the scent of damp earth and fresh pine as Sir Cedric walked through the wooded path leading to the ancient ruins. His boots sank slightly into the soft ground, each step a silent testament to centuries of stories buried underfoot. The ruins, remnants of a castle long forgotten by time, were said to house relics of King Arthur and his knights.

Cedric, a historian by training and an explorer at heart, has always been fascinated by the evolution of myths—how objects like Excalibur transitioned from mundane iron to symbols of divine authority. Today, he hopes to uncover artifacts to provide insight into this transformation.

He paused by a crumbling stone wall, tracing his fingers over the moss-covered blocks. Coolness seeped through his gloves as he imagined knights walking these same grounds, their lives governed by the power vested in their swords. The sword wasn't just a weapon but a key to understanding societal values and belief shifts.

As he ventured deeper into what was once a grand hall, Cedric thought about how Excalibur's narrative mirrored societal changes. Initially just another sword, it became enveloped in magic and mystery as storytellers across ages wove tales that reflected their times' needs for heroes who were more than mere men. They needed legends.

A rustle from the nearby thicket snapped him out of his reverie. A deer, startled by his presence, dashed through the underbrush, leaving behind a whispering echo. Cedric smiled faintly; even wildlife seemed to tread cautiously around these sacred relics of past eras.

He knelt near where the old throne might have stood, gently brushing leaves and dirt away with his hand. His fingers touched something hard and metallic—not a sword, but a small cross-shaped brooch possibly worn by a high-ranking knight or royalty. This tiny piece could suggest religious influences on Arthurian legends or hint at political motivations cloaked in piety and chivalry.

Holding it up to the light filtering through the canopy above, Cedric felt connected across time to those who shaped these narratives. What did they think as they spun tales that turned history into legend? Was it awe or a calculated move to inspire people during turbulent times?

As he carefully placed the brooch into his bag for further examination back at his lab, Cedric pondered how today's society romanticizes historical figures and events, much like medieval storytellers did with Excalibur. Are we looking for modern-day Arthurs?

Would understanding our fascination with turning history into legend reveal more about our current values and beliefs?

FROM MUNDANE METAL to Magical Might: The Evolution of Excalibur

The story of Excalibur is shrouded not just in the mist of Avalon but in the veils of history sage mythology, intertwining to form a narrative that has captivated audiences for centuries. This legendary sword, known for its supernatural prowess and divine symbolism, embarked on its journey through the annals of Arthurian lore as a somewhat ordinary weapon. Excalibur transformed through the changing tides of cultural and political climates, reflecting broader societal shifts that romanticized history and legend. Here, we peel back these layers to reveal how Excalibur evolved from a mere battle implement to a symbol of ultimate authority and righteousness.

The narrative significance of Excalibur has undergone profound transformations, shaping and being shaped by the societal values and historical contexts of different periods. Initially mentioned in early texts like those by Geoffrey of Monmouth, the sword's origins were far less mystical. Understanding this metamorphosis provides insight into the art of storytelling and the collective psyche of societies that altered these tales over centuries.

As we delve into this exploration, we will examine **how different eras have influenced** the legend of Excalibur. The sword's journey from a functional weapon possibly crafted by an ordinary smith to a magical entity bestowed by the Lady of the Lake encapsulates shifts in narrative driven primarily by audience expectations and prevailing cultural narratives.

This transformation is not merely about changing literary motifs but is deeply embedded in the **political climate** of various times. Each rendition of Excalibur's tale mirrors contemporary issues, imbuing the sword with an ever-greater significance as it becomes a tool for legitimizing divine right and heroic idealism. Through this lens, we can observe how legends reinforce or challenge contemporary values and leadership traits deemed essential during different historical moments.

Furthermore, this chapter sets the stage for understanding how such legendary narratives contribute to our modern interpretation of history and myth. By analyzing these changes, we gain insights into how societies use legends to forge identities and idealize past figures according to present needs.

The broader implications of this exploration are vast. They invite us to reflect on how our current values influence the reinterpretation of historical and mythical figures today. Are we, like the bards and scribes of yore, molding our legends to fit contemporary paradigms?

In this book, we aim to uncover the factual layers beneath the Arthurian romances and provide a balanced view that respects historical accuracy and myth's power. By bridging these realms, readers can fully appreciate Excalibur's legendary narrative and its historical underpinnings.

This introductory chapter paves the way for a deeper investigation into what changes occurred in telling Excalibur's story and why these changes happened. As we move forward, remember that our journey is one not just through history but through the evolving human condition itself—reflecting on how our ancestors viewed their world and how those views shape our present perceptions.

Excalibur, the legendary sword of King Arthur, has undergone a remarkable transformation in its narrative significance throughout history. Initially depicted as a powerful weapon without magical attributes, Excalibur became a symbol of divine right and heroism in later Arthurian tales. This shift from a mundane object to a supernatural symbol reflects the changing expectations of audiences over time. As stories surrounding Excalibur adapted to meet the desires of different cultural and political climates, the sword's significance grew from a simple tool of war to a mystical emblem embodying ideals of chivalry and nobility.

In early texts such as those by Geoffrey of Monmouth, Excalibur was portrayed as an exceptional weapon granted to King Arthur, setting him apart as a heroic figure destined for greatness. However, it lacked the magical qualities commonly associated with later iterations of the sword. Over time, as societal values shifted and audiences craved more fantastical elements in their tales, Excalibur's narrative evolved to include magical properties like being bestowed by the Lady of the Lake or having the power to confer kingship upon its wielder.

The evolution of Excalibur's narrative significance highlights how storytelling adapts to meet the desires and expectations of its audience. What was once a straightforward weapon became infused with supernatural elements to captivate imaginations and elevate King Arthur's stature. This metamorphosis speaks to the power of myth and legend in shaping cultural narratives and reflecting societal values to its people.

Continue reading to explore how cultural and political climates influenced Excalibur's storytelling over different periods.

Cultural and Political Influences on Excalibur's Storytelling

Throughout history, the tale of Excalibur has been shaped by the cultural and political landscapes of the times. The evolution of Excalibur's narrative significance from a mundane object to a supernatural symbol is intricately tied to the societal expectations and beliefs prevalent during different periods. In early texts like those by Geoffrey of Monmouth, Excalibur was portrayed as a mighty sword. Still, it lacked the mystical attributes commonly associated with it today. **As societies evolved and storytelling became more intertwined with magic and legend elements, Excalibur became a symbol of divine right and heroism.**

Influence of Cultural Shifts

Cultural shifts played a significant role in altering Excalibur's perception. As societies embraced more fantastical elements in their narratives, the sword of King Arthur became imbued with magical properties. **The allure of mystical tales captivated audiences**, leading to the incorporation of supernatural elements into the story of Excalibur. This shift not only entertained but also elevated the legendary status of King Arthur and his trusted weapon.

Political Machinations

Moreover, political climates also influenced how Excalibur was depicted in various retellings. During political unrest or upheaval, **the symbolism of Excalibur as a tool of leadership and legitimacy became** particularly pronounced. The sword came to represent not just a weapon but a source of authority and power, reflecting the aspirations and struggles for control prevalent in society then.

Reflecting Societal Values

The changes in Excalibur's portrayal mirror broader societal values and aspirations across different historical periods. Excalibur became a beacon of hope and righteousness when societies sought heroes and symbols of greatness. The sword symbolized physical strength and moral fortitude, aligning with the ideals held dear by communities seeking inspiration and guidance.

Adaptation to Audience Expectations

As storytelling evolved to cater to changing audience tastes, so too did the depiction of Excalibur. The sword's metamorphosis from a mere weapon to a mythical artifact was driven by **the desire to enchant and enthrall listeners** with tales that transcended reality. By weaving elements of magic and destiny into the narrative, storytellers captured the imagination of their audiences, ensuring that Excalibur remained a timeless symbol of heroism and virtue.

Interplay Between Culture, Politics, and Narrative

The interplay between culture, politics, and narrative is evident in how Excalibur's story has been crafted over centuries. **Each retelling reflects not just the values and beliefs of the storyteller but also the desires and fears prevalent in society at that time.** By examining these influences, we can gain deeper insights into how legends like that of Excalibur continue to resonate with audiences today.

In understanding how cultural and political climates have shaped the storytelling surrounding Excalibur, we unravel not just a mythical tale but also **a reflection of humanity's eternal quest for meaning,** purpose, and transcendence through storytelling.

The evolution of Excalibur from a mere weapon to a symbol of divine right and heroism mirrors broader societal shifts toward romanticizing history. As cultures transformed and narratives evolved,

Excalibur's significance morphed into a potent emblem of power and destiny.

Historically, societies have often imbued objects with mystical or legendary qualities to elevate their heroes and legends. The transformation of Excalibur reflects this tendency to mythologize historical artifacts and figures, shaping them into larger-than-life symbols that resonate with the values and aspirations of each era.

The metamorphosis of Excalibur highlights society's yearning for magical elements in their historical narratives. The desire for enchantment and wonder grew as civilizations progressed, leading to the embellishment of stories like King Arthur and his legendary sword. **By infusing Excalibur with supernatural powers, storytellers captured the imaginations of audiences hungry for tales of bravery and charisma.** This shift from mundane objects to mystical artifacts demonstrates how storytelling adapts to meet its listeners' changing needs and desires.

The romanticization of Excalibur also reflects society's evolving values and beliefs. The sword took on new meanings in different periods that aligned with the prevailing ideologies and cultural norms. **As societies embraced the ideals of chivalry, honor, and nobility, Excalibur became a potent symbol that embodied these virtues.** The sword became not just a tool for battle but a representation of noble lineage, rightful kingship, and heroic destiny.

The allure of Excalibur lies in its ability to transcend the confines of reality and tap into the realm of myth and legend. By transforming a simple sword into an object of mystical power, storytellers elevated the ordinary into the extraordinary, captivating audiences with tales of magic and destiny. **This transformation speaks to humanity's eternal quest for meaning and purpose** as we seek to imbue our lives with significance beyond the mundane.

We can glimpse how societies shape their histories to reflect their values and aspirations through the lens of Excalibur's evolution.

The sword's journey from a mundane object to a supernatural symbol illustrates how narratives can be crafted to inspire, enchant, and unite communities under shared ideals. **In embracing the legend of Excalibur, we embrace not just a story but a reflection of our collective longing for greatness and transcendence.**

As we delve into the saga of Excalibur, it becomes evident that this legendary sword is more than just a piece of metal; it is a profound symbol shaped by the ebbs and flows of human culture and political climates. **Understanding the evolution** of Excalibur from a simple weapon to a supernatural icon reveals much about our own transformations in perceiving history and myth. This transformation is not merely about a sword. Still, it reflects a broader societal shift towards romanticizing our past, making it crucial for us to explore these narratives critically.

Exploring how cultural and political climates have influenced Excalibur's story reveals a mirror reflecting our changing values and beliefs over time. These shifts in storytelling were not arbitrary but driven by the needs and expectations of people across different epochs, revealing the power of narrative in shaping and reshaping societal identity.

By **analyzing Excalibur's metamorphosis** within the context of broader societal changes, we gain insights into the dynamic interaction between history and legend. This sword's journey from the mundane to the magical is about aesthetic changes and how societies use myths to forge identity, inspire heroes, and instill moral values.

This chapter sets the stage for a deeper exploration into the legends of Excalibur and Merlin, encouraging you to question and understand the narratives that have long been taken at face value. As we continue this journey together, I invite you to remain curious and reflective, challenging what you know and embracing the revelations that lie ahead. The stories of Excalibur and Merlin are not just tales of old but are keys to understanding the past and its impact on our present and future.

Let us move forward with an open mind and an eager heart, ready to uncover more truths behind these captivating legends. Your engagement with this exploration will enrich your knowledge and deepen your appreciation for how our histories are crafted and remembered. Together, let's turn the pages with anticipation, ready to be inspired by the powerful lessons embedded in these age-old stories.

Chapter 2: The Many Faces of Merlin

In the dim light of the early morning, Thomas, a seasoned historian specializing in medieval studies, sat at his cluttered desk surrounded by towering stacks of ancient manuscripts and modern texts. The faint aroma of musty paper filled the air, mingling with the sharp scent of ink as he poured over a particularly well-worn copy of Geoffrey of Monmouth's "Historia Regum Britanniae." His eyes traced the lines where Merlin's tales unfolded, a character as enigmatic as the dawn that slowly dispelled the shadows in his cramped study.

Outside, the world was waking up; birds chirped tentatively, their songs barely audible through the thick stone walls of his university office. Yet inside, time stood still as Thomas delved deeper into understanding how historical figures like Myrddin and Ambrosius had merged into this singular, mythical embodiment known as Merlin. Each page turn seemed to whisper secrets from centuries past that Thomas was determined to decode.

As he sifted through various accounts and legends, he wondered why these amalgamations occurred. Was it merely the passage of time that blended these figures together, or was there a more profound societal need that these stories addressed? The thought nagged at him like a persistent wind tugging at frail branches. He pondered how Merlin's evolving identity served different purposes over time—shifting from a madman in Welsh legends to a sage advisor in Arthurian romance.

A sudden gust rattled the windowpane, drawing Thomas's attention momentarily away from his books. He watched as leaves danced wildly in the wind outside—a chaotic yet rhythmic spectacle. It reminded him how narratives, too, are tossed and turned by the winds of cultural change and retelling. Returning to his texts with renewed vigor, he noted connections between political climates and narrative evolutions, how kings and clergy might have influenced which version of Merlin persisted through history.

Each document before him told part of a story but left much untold. How did people relate to Merlin during different eras? Did they see him as we do now, or did his magical qualities serve as more of a metaphor for wisdom and guidance? These questions spun around in Thomas's mind as he tried piecing together fragments of texts and societal beliefs encapsulated within them.

As dusk began to claim the day, casting long shadows across his cluttered desk, Thomas leaned back in his chair. His eyes were tired, but his spirit was alight with ideas and theories waiting to be penned down. The connection between myth and history is often obscured by time's passing fog—could he perhaps clear some of it away?

What does our fascination with characters like Merlin tell us about our desires for magic and wisdom in leadership?

Unraveling the Enigma: Who Really Was Merlin?

Merlin, the iconic wizard of Arthurian legend, has long been depicted as a wise and mysterious figure wielding magic and prophecy. Yet, this singular image belies a far more complex origin story—a tapestry woven from various historical and mythical strands that have evolved over centuries. In our exploration, we will dissect these layers to reveal not just one but many of Merlin's faces.

Merlin's persona is not merely a product of creative storytelling but a deliberate synthesis of multiple characters from history and mythology. This blending highlights his adaptability, allowing him to remain relevant as narratives and societal values shift through the ages.

By understanding these origins, readers can appreciate Merlin as a fixture in Arthurian romance and a symbol of cultural evolution.

The first layer to unravel involves identifying the key figures contributing to Merlin's multifaceted identity. Historical figures like Ambrosius Aurelianus, a Roman-British war leader, provide the roots for Merlin's leadership and strategic qualities. Meanwhile, elements of Celtic mythology introduce aspects of magic and nature that are now synonymous with his character.

The reasons behind this amalgamation are as fascinating as they are insightful. Merging these figures served multiple purposes—enhancing the dramatic appeal of the narratives, embedding desired moral lessons, and aligning with prevailing religious and cultural contexts. This strategic blending also allowed Merlin to transcend his origins, becoming a universal symbol whose wisdom and power could speak to audiences across different eras.

Evaluating how Merlin's evolving identity impacts his role in Arthurian literature brings us to reflect on the nature of myth-making itself. As Merlin transformed from a composite character into a singular sage, his role expanded beyond the confines of individual stories. He became an archetype embodying wisdom, guidance, and foresight—qualities that resonate deeply with our human experience.

This chapter promises to be both an exploration and a celebration of Merlin's complex heritage. Through it, we aim not only to illuminate the origins of this legendary figure but also to understand how mythologies develop and gain significance in cultural consciousness.

By peering into the historical tapestry that forms Merlin's identity, we gain more than just knowledge about a legendary figure; we uncover insights about ourselves and how we create heroes who encapsulate our highest ideals. This journey into the past enriches our understanding of literature's power to shape enduring legends that continue to inspire and instruct us across generations.

Merlin, the iconic wizard of Arthurian legend, is not a singular creation but a composite character drawn from various historical and mythical figures. His identity is a rich tapestry woven from different threads of folklore and history, each contributing to his complex persona. One key figure contributing to Merlin's composite identity is the Welsh bard Myrddin. Myrddin, known for his prophetic powers and association with the wilds of nature, laid the foundation for Merlin's mystical and enigmatic character. Through the centuries, elements of Myrddin's lore were intertwined with other figures to shape Merlin into the wise and magical advisor we know today.

Another significant influence on Merlin's character is the historical figure Ambrosius. Ambrosius, a Romano-British war leader who fought against Saxon invaders in the 5th century, provided the archetype of a powerful and strategic leader. This aspect of Ambrosius was blended with Myrddin's prophetic abilities to create a character who wielded magic and possessed keen insight and political acumen. The amalgamation of these traits from different figures resulted in

Merlin embodying wisdom, magic, prophecy, and leadership qualities in Arthurian literature.

In addition to Myrddin and Ambrosius, other mythological figures such as Lailoken and Emrys also shaped Merlin's character. Lailoken, a Scottish wildman known for his madness and prophetic visions, added an element of mystique and unpredictability to Merlin's persona. Emrys, a name associated with Merlin in Welsh texts, highlighted his connection to ancient Celtic traditions and emphasized his role as a bridge between the old ways and the new Christian order.

Fusing these historical and mythical figures into Merlin's composite identity speaks to the fluid nature of storytelling and mythmaking. Over time, as different cultures interacted and narratives evolved, Merlin evolved as well, adapting to fit the needs and desires of each era. This transformation allowed Merlin to become a versatile symbol in Arthurian literature, embodying not just one fixed set of traits but a myriad of characteristics that made him a timeless and compelling figure.

Read on to discover how these varied influences converged to create the multifaceted character of Merlin in Arthurian lore.

Throughout history, the character of Merlin has evolved through a process of amalgamation, combining various historical and mythical figures into a single, complex persona. **The reasons behind this amalgamation are multifaceted and reveal the adaptability and versatility of Merlin as a symbol in Arthurian literature.** One significant reason for this blending of figures is the **desire to create a multidimensional character** who embodies different qualities and virtues. By incorporating elements from diverse sources, Merlin becomes a rich tapestry of wisdom, magic, and prophecy, appealing to various audiences.

Another reason for the amalgamation is the need to adapt Merlin to fit changing narratives and theological beliefs over time. As societies evolved and different cultures contributed to the Arthurian legends, Merlin transformed to reflect these shifting ideologies. By drawing on various historical and mythical figures, storytellers could mold Merlin into a character that resonated with contemporary audiences, ensuring his relevance across centuries.

Furthermore, the amalgamation of different figures into Merlin enhances the mystique and enigma surrounding his character. By weaving together multiple identities, Merlin becomes a figure shrouded in mystery and intrigue, captivating readers and listeners alike with his complex nature. This aura of mystery adds depth to Merlin's character, making him more compelling and engaging as a central figure in Arthurian tales.

The amalgamation also allows for greater storytelling possibilities, as Merlin's composite identity provides writers with a wealth of material to draw upon. By incorporating traits from various historical and mythical sources, authors can create intricate plotlines and nuanced character development, enriching the overall narrative of the Arthurian legends.

Moreover, merging different figures into Merlin helps to blur the lines between history and myth, creating a character that straddles both realms seamlessly. This blending of fact and fiction adds an element of intrigue to Merlin's character, inviting readers to explore the boundaries between reality and imagination within the context of Arthurian literature.

In essence, **the amalgamation of historical and mythical figures into the character of Merlin serves to make him a dynamic and multifaceted persona**. By drawing on diverse sources, storytellers have crafted a figure who embodies wisdom, magic, prophecy, mystery, and more, ensuring that Merlin remains a timeless symbol in Arthurian lore. This synthesis of identities not only enriches the character but also underscores Merlin's enduring appeal and adaptability throughout the ages.

Merlin's evolving identity plays a crucial role in shaping the narrative landscape of Arthurian literature. As a versatile symbol of wisdom, magic, and prophecy, Merlin embodies the complexities of human nature and the eternal struggle between light and darkness. Through the amalgamation of various historical and mythical figures, Merlin emerges as a multifaceted character with depth and nuance, captivating readers with his enigmatic persona.

In Arthurian literature, Merlin's character bridges the mundane and the mystical, guiding King Arthur and the audience through trials and tribulations. His evolving identity reflects the changing tides of storytelling traditions, adapting to suit new narratives and theological interpretations. This adaptability allows Merlin to remain relevant across centuries, resonating with audiences seeking guidance and wisdom in tumultuous times.

As a figure shrouded in mystery and magic, Merlin captivates readers with his otherworldly abilities and profound insights. His presence in Arthurian tales adds an element of wonder and enchantment, elevating the stories beyond mere historical accounts into realms of myth and legend. Through Merlin's evolving identity, authors have been able to explore themes of destiny, power, and sacrifice, enriching the tapestry of Arthurian literature with layers of complexity.

Merlin's impact on Arthurian literature extends beyond his wise counselor or magical advisor role. His character embodies the timeless struggle between good and evil, offering readers a glimpse into the complexities of human nature and the consequences of choice. By delving into Merlin's evolving identity, audiences can uncover deeper truths about themselves and their place in the world, prompting introspection and self-discovery.

The evolution of Merlin's character mirrors the evolution of storytelling itself, showcasing how narratives can adapt to reflect societal values and beliefs. As readers engage with different iterations of Merlin across various texts, they are invited to ponder the nature of truth, myth, and legend. Through this exploration, audiences can gain a deeper appreciation for the power of storytelling to illuminate universal truths and inspire personal growth.

Merlin's presence in Arthurian literature is a beacon of hope in times of darkness, offering readers solace and guidance amidst chaos and uncertainty. His evolving identity reminds us that change is inevitable, but growth is optional. By embracing the lessons embedded within Merlin's character, readers can navigate their own journeys with courage and wisdom, drawing inspiration from his timeless teachings on love, loyalty, and honor.

In conclusion, Throughout Arthurian literature, Merlin stands as a testament to the enduring power of storytelling to shape our understanding of ourselves and the world around us.

Merlin's character, a mosaic of historical and mythical influences, encapsulates a depth beyond traditional storytelling's surface. By identifying the figures contributing to this composite identity, we recognize Merlin as a wizard and a repository of cultural narratives and beliefs spanning centuries. This synthesis reflects an evolutionary process in storytelling where characters adapt to meet the needs of their time, providing relevance and resonance across generations.

The amalgamation of figures like the Welsh bard Myrddin and the historical Ambrosius into Merlin's character highlights a crucial literary narrative technique: **adaptation**. This blending serves more than just filling gaps in a story; it indicates a more extensive cultural practice where stories are continuously woven into the fabric of societal values and historical contexts. Thus, Merlin becomes a symbol not just of wisdom and magic but also of legends' adaptability and enduring nature.

Evaluating how Merlin's evolving identity impacts his role in Arthurian literature opens up broader discussions about the function of myth and legend in human culture. Merlin's character bridges the past and the present, allowing contemporary audiences to explore ancient wisdom through modern eyes. His role in literature is not static but dynamic, changing as our understanding and interpretation of these myths evolve.

Reflecting on these insights encourages us to appreciate the layered complexities of legendary figures like Merlin. It invites us to consider how our interpretations of these characters shape our understanding of history, morality, and human nature. As we move forward in this book, let us carry with us the knowledge that legends like those of Merlin are more than just stories; they are mirrors reflecting our collective human experience, imbued with the power to inspire, teach, and transform.

Chapter 3: Unmasking the Legend: The Truth Behind Arthurian Romance

In the dim light of a late afternoon, Thomas, a young university professor, strolled through the ancient corridors of the library. His mind was preoccupied with Arthurian legends, not merely as tales of chivalry and magic but as mirrors reflecting the distorted images of medieval truths. The weight of these thoughts made his steps heavy against the stone floor.

He paused by a window, watching how the light played on the glass—fragmented yet beautiful. It reminded him of Geoffrey of Monmouth's writings, fragmented pieces of history embellished into beautiful narratives. Thomas often wondered how much truth was sacrificed for beauty or if they could ever be entwined without losing one to the other.

As he returned to his search among the shelves, his fingers brushed against the spines of aged books, each carrying whispers from centuries past. He pulled out a particularly worn volume titled "Historia Regum Britanniae" and flipped through its pages slowly. Here was Geoffrey's hand blending myth with history, perhaps aware that future scholars would wrestle with discerning fact from fiction.

A student approached him hesitantly, breaking his train of thought. She asked about King Arthur's historical impact versus his literary mythos. As he explained the layers of legend and historical context, Thomas felt a familiar thrill—the dance between knowing and imagining what might have been.

Later, sitting at an old wooden desk bathed in the orange glow from an overhead lamp that seemed too tired to shine brightly, Thomas scribbled notes for his next lecture. The room smelled faintly of dust and old paper—a comfort to him. His notes were meticulous, yet he questioned every source: What did people believe about their history? How did these beliefs shape their understanding of themselves and their past?

As he packed up to leave, the quiet hum of the library enveloped him once more. The echo of his footsteps filled the space as if to prove that he was there—among legends, between truths and myths.

Why do we choose beauty over truth in our histories, and does this choice change how we see our present?

Peeling Back the Layers of Arthurian Glamour

The tales of King Arthur and his Knights of the Round Table have enchanted audiences for centuries, weaving a tapestry rich with chivalric quests, heroic deeds, and magical enchantments. Yet, beneath these captivating narratives lies a complex layer of historical truth that often remains overshadowed by their romantic allure. This chapter aims to demystify the Arthurian legends, stripping away the romanticization to reveal the medieval realities they cloak.

With its knights and noble quests, Arthurian romance presents a seductive picture of the medieval era. However, this portrayal is not without its distortions. The embellishments that make these stories so compelling can also lead to skewed perceptions of history. By dissecting how these narratives have been romanticized, we see their impact on our understanding of the past.

Primary sources like Geoffrey of Monmouth's "Historia Regum Britanniae" (The History of the Kings of Britain) are invaluable in this pursuit. Although Geoffrey's work is not devoid of mythical elements, it is one of the earliest attempts to chronicle the legends surrounding

Arthur and his court. Analyzing such texts helps us sift fact from fiction, providing a clearer picture of the era than most modern retellings offer.

The dramatic embellishments found in Arthurian tales are not merely entertaining; they mold our contemporary views of medieval society. By understanding these fabrications, we can better appreciate the truths and fabrications within these stories. This chapter will explore how recognizing these distinctions enhances our comprehension of historical narratives and challenges our preconceived notions about the past.

Furthermore, this analysis is not just academic—it has real-world implications on how history is taught and understood. Misconceptions about medieval times are pervasive in popular culture, influencing everything from educational materials to media portrayals. By confronting these myths with factual analysis, we aim to contribute to a more nuanced understanding of history.

Throughout this exploration, we will also reflect on what the persistent appeal of Arthurian legends says about our cultural values and ideals. Why do these stories endure? What needs do they fulfill? We will gain insight into historical facts and the human condition by examining these questions.

Thus, let us venture into this inquiry with curiosity and skepticism, prepared to uncover truths that are as enlightening as they are essential. In doing so, we pay homage to the richness of medieval culture and equip ourselves with a more discerning eye for distinguishing historical fact from fanciful fiction.

The romanticization of Arthurian legends has long captivated audiences, weaving tales of heroism, chivalry, and magic that have become synonymous with the medieval era. However, beneath the enchanting veneer lies a complex web of historical truths often obscured by dramatic embellishments. While adding flair to the stories, these embellishments can distort our perceptions of the actual events and figures from that time. Peeling back the layers of fantasy to uncover the core truths hidden within these legendary narratives is crucial.

When we immerse ourselves in the world of Arthurian romance, we are transported to a realm where knights embark on noble quests, wizards wield powerful spells, and love conquers all. Yet, amidst these fantastical elements lies a rich tapestry of historical context that is often overshadowed by the allure of myth and legend. By examining the romanticized versions of these tales, we can unravel the threads of truth woven into the fabric of Arthurian lore.

The romanticized portrayals of King Arthur and his knights have shaped our collective imagination, painting a picture of an idyllic past filled with grandeur and gallantry. However, behind the shining armor and majestic castles lies a more nuanced reality marked by political intrigue, social upheaval, and cultural evolution. By peeling back the layers of romanticism surrounding these figures, we can better understand their challenges and impact on medieval society.

As we delve into the world of Arthurian romance, it becomes apparent that **the line between fact and fiction is often blurred.** Legendary figures like Merlin and Guinevere take on larger-than-life personas in these tales, their deeds exaggerated for dramatic effect. Separating reality from myth requires a critical eye and a willingness to look beyond the surface-level narratives passed down through generations.

We can unravel the medieval era's complexities by examining how **the romanticization of Arthurian legends distorts our perceptions** of history. It is essential to approach these stories with a discerning gaze, questioning the motives behind their embellishments and seeking out the kernels of truth buried within. Only then can we gain a more accurate understanding of this fascinating historical period?

Continue reading as we delve deeper into primary sources like Geoffrey of Monmouth's works to uncover a more nuanced perspective on medieval history.

Geoffrey of Monmouth's works serve as a pivotal source for unraveling the intricate tapestry of Arthurian legends, offering valuable insights into the historical and cultural context of the medieval period. Through a critical analysis of Geoffrey's writings, we can peel back the layers of embellishment and fantasy that have shrouded the true essence of Arthurian tales. **Geoffrey's meticulous detailing of lineage, battles, and political landscapes provides a more grounded perspective on the era in which these legends were born.**

In delving into Geoffrey's accounts, we encounter a world where history intertwines with mythology, blurring the lines between fact and fiction. **His vivid descriptions of Arthur's conquests and reign offer a glimpse into the political landscape of early Britain, showcasing power struggles, alliances, and betrayals that shaped the destiny of kingdoms.** By immersing ourselves in Geoffrey's narratives, we can discern the underlying truths that inspired later generations to craft grandiose tales of chivalry and magic.

Geoffrey's portrayal of Merlin as a wise advisor and visionary figure sheds light on the importance of counsel and foresight in tumultuous times. Through his characterizations, we understand how medieval societies valued wisdom and strategic thinking in navigating complex political landscapes. **Merlin's enigmatic presence symbolizes hope and guidance amidst chaos and uncertainty**, resonating with audiences across centuries.

Moreover, Geoffrey's accounts highlight the role of storytelling in shaping cultural identities and preserving historical legacies. **The oral traditions that inspired Geoffrey's writings underscore the significance of narrative in transmitting knowledge and values from one generation to the next.** By studying Geoffrey's texts, we uncover historical truths and appreciate the enduring power of storytelling in connecting the past, present, and future.

Exploring Geoffrey of Monmouth's primary sources confronts us with a nuanced portrayal of medieval history that challenges conventional perceptions shaped by romanticized retellings. **By engaging critically with Geoffrey's works, we can discern the threads of truth woven into the fabric of Arthurian legends.** We will better appreciate the complexities and contradictions that define this rich tapestry of stories.

Analytical Framework

The framework presented in this chapter offers a structured approach to unraveling the layers of romantic embellishments in Arthurian legends and understanding their impact on contemporary perceptions of the medieval era. By breaking down the components of this model, readers can navigate the complexities of legendary tales with a critical eye toward historical truths.

Identifying Common Romantic Themes

The first step in the framework involves **identifying common romantic themes** prevalent in Arthurian legends. Themes such as heroism, chivalry, and magic often dominate these tales, shaping our perception of the medieval period. By recognizing these recurring motifs, readers can separate the fantastical elements from potentially historical events or practices.

Comparing Themes Against Historical Realism

Once readers have identified these romantic themes, the next step is to **compare them against historical accounts** and known cultural practices of the Middle Ages. This critical analysis allows a deeper understanding of how these themes align with or diverge from historical realities. By juxtaposing legend with history, readers can discern where embellishments may have distorted our knowledge of the past.

Evaluating Sources and Biases

A crucial aspect of this framework involves **evaluating the sources** of Arthurian legends, mainly works like Geoffrey of Monmouth's "Historia Regum Britanniae." Understanding the authors' biases, intentions, and the context in which these stories were written provides valuable insights into how and why certain embellishments were introduced. By scrutinizing the origins of these tales, readers can uncover layers of interpretation that have shaped our contemporary views.

Synthesizing Information for Clarity

The final step in this framework calls for **synthesizing all** gathered information to differentiate between romanticized aspects and likely historical truths. By combining insights from previous steps, readers can develop a nuanced understanding of Arthurian narratives that balance myth with reality. This synthesis empowers individuals to engage critically with legendary material and appreciate the complexities of separating fact from fiction.

Practical Implications and Application

This framework equips readers with the tools necessary to navigate the intricate tapestry of Arthurian legends with a discerning eye. By applying this analytical model, individuals can gain a deeper appreciation for the historical context underlying these tales and challenge prevailing misconceptions about the medieval era. Ultimately, this framework encourages critical engagement with legendary material, fostering a more informed and nuanced perspective on medieval history.

In summary, by following this structured approach to dissecting Arthurian legends, readers can untangle the web of romantic embellishments that have shaped our understanding of the medieval era. Through careful analysis and thoughtful reflection, individuals can uncover hidden truths within legendary tales and appreciate the rich tapestry of history that lies beneath the surface.

Unmasking the allure of Arthurian romance requires a meticulous deconstruction of the layers of myth that have shrouded the true medieval essence. This process enriches our understanding and recalibrates our perception of history.

Step 1: Assessing the Impact of Romanticization on Arthurian Legends

First, grasp the **concept of romanticization and** its potent effect on distorting historical truths. Delve into the embellishments that paint Arthurian legends with broad strokes of chivalry and courtly love, recognizing how these narratives shape our view of a bygone era. The portrayal of King Arthur as an idealized figure is a prime example of romanticization that needs critical examination for its far-reaching implications, including the perpetuation of stereotypes and crafting an unrealistic medieval fantasy.

Step 2: Uncovering Historical Context through Primary Sources

Primary sources like Geoffrey of Monmouth's writings are invaluable in providing a more accurate **contextual understanding** of Arthurian legends. Engage deeply with these texts, mindful of the author's biases and the historical circumstances under which they were penned. This careful analysis is crucial in separating historical figures from their legendary counterparts and understanding the actual political climate of the Arthurian period.

Step 3: Understanding the Role of Dramatic Embellishments

Dramatic embellishments in Arthurian literature often stem from a desire to entertain or impart moral lessons. Recognize these motivations and assess their impact on contemporary views of the medieval era. This awareness helps develop a **critical eye** for distinguishing between narrative flourishes and factual historical information, especially in popular representations of knights, wizards and quests like that for the Holy Grail.

Step 4: Debunking Myths and Clarifying Historical Truths

It is essential to challenge prevalent myths, such as the literal existence of King Arthur or magical elements like Excalibur. Employ **critical thinking** and thorough research to debunk these myths, relying on reputable sources and scholarly research to verify what is historically accurate. This step is fundamental in presenting a more truthful depiction of the Arthurian era.

Step 5: Reflecting on the Implications of Historical Distortions

Finally, reflect on how romanticized versions of Arthurian legends influence literature, popular culture, and public perceptions. Analyze the consequences of these distortions on our overall understanding of history. Promoting a balanced view that honors the enchanting narratives and the historical truths of the Arthurian legends is crucial.

This structured approach demystifies the enthralling tales of King Arthur and his knights. It reinstates the importance of historical accuracy in understanding our past. By embracing this methodical exploration, we move closer to a comprehensive appreciation of the legend and the truth, ensuring that the enchantment of Arthurian romance enhances rather than obscures our historical consciousness.

Chapter 4: Cross-Examining Camelot: A Comparative Textual Analysis

In the dimly lit library of an ancient manor house nestled in the heart of Cornwall, Eleanor sat surrounded by leather-bound volumes that whispered tales of yore. The musty air was thick with the scent of old paper and wood polish, a testament to generations who had sought knowledge within these walls. Her fingers traced the intricate spine of a book titled *The Legends of King Arthur and His Knights*, her eyes scanning lines steeped in mystery and magic.

Outside, the wind howled like the distant cries of medieval warriors, rattling the lead-lined windows as if trying to get a glimpse of the secrets unfolding within. Eleanor's mind wandered through forests dense with myth and fog, where mystical forces bestowed Excalibur upon Arthur. This contrasted starkly with another text in which the sword lay in stone, awaiting a worthy hand.

She pondered deeply on Merlin's powers as described across texts—some spoke of him as a wizard influencing kings and battles with profound wisdom; others painted him as almost omnipotent, meddling with time itself. These disparities gnawed at her, feeding into her broader quest for truth amidst legends beautifully woven into Britain's cultural fabric.

Her thoughts were interrupted by a creaking noise as Mrs. Penrose entered bearing a tray with tea and biscuits—the aroma mingling peculiarly with that of ancient parchment. "Storm's picking up," Mrs. Penrose noted, setting down the tray. Eleanor nodded absently, her mind still entwined with knights and enchantments.

"Thank you," she murmured before turning back to her books. She was sipping tea that scorched slightly against her lips but warmed her insides—a fleeting comfort against the chill that seeped through every crevice of the old house.

As night deepened around her, shadows danced across stone walls lined with portraits whose eyes seemed to follow Eleanor's every move. Candlelight flickered against their faces painted centuries ago, silent witnesses to history's unending dialogue between fact and fiction.

Why do we cling so ardently to legends like Arthur and his knights? Does their transformation reveal more about us than it does about them over time?

PEELING BACK THE LAYERS of Legend

In the sprawling tapestry of Arthurian legends, the figures of Excalibur and Merlin stand out, woven with threads of magic and mystery. Yet, as we dig deeper into these narratives, a compelling question arises: **how much of what we read is rooted in historical truth, and how much is the embellishment of imaginative minds?** This exploration seeks to dissect various Arthurian texts to sift fact from poetic fiction, offering a clearer view of these legendary figures.

Arthurian legends have been retold across generations, each author painting their own hues onto the stories. The origins of Excalibur and the extent of Merlin's powers vary significantly across texts. Such discrepancies not only reflect the personal biases and cultural backgrounds of the authors but also their distinct narrative intentions. By comparing these stories side by side, we aim to uncover underlying truths that have been obscured by centuries of retelling.

Unveiling Historical Threads

The task at hand involves a meticulous examination of different Arthurian accounts. We'll look at how each version handles critical elements like the magical sword Excalibur—was it given by the Lady of the Lake or forged by an otherworldly force? Similarly, Merlin's portrayal as a wise sage or a manipulative wizard changes dramatically depending on the text. This comparative approach highlights inconsistencies and helps pinpoint consistent elements, suggesting a kernel of historical truth beneath the layers of lore.

Navigating Through Narratives

Understanding why each author might alter or emphasize certain aspects over others involves delving into their historical and cultural contexts, often influencing how characters and events are depicted. For instance, medieval authors might have imbued their tales with chivalric ideals. At the same time, later writers could have altered narratives to suit more contemporary themes or moral lessons.

Crafting a Comparative Lens

We will also discuss methodologies for conducting systematic comparisons across texts. This isn't just about reading and noting differences. It involves critically analyzing why these differences exist and what they tell us about societal values and historical contexts at the time of writing. By employing a structured comparative analysis, we can discern which aspects of the legends are likely embellished and which may be anchored in actual historical events or figures.

This chapter does not just revisit tales old as time; it reevaluates them through a scholarly lens, encouraging readers to look beyond the enchanting surface. The aim is to empower enthusiasts and scholars alike to recognize and appreciate the historical roots and artistic flourishes within Arthurian legends.

Through this detailed inquiry, we embark on a journey that promises deeper understanding and renewed appreciation for one of history's most captivating narratives. By engaging with these legendary figures analytically, we connect with our past through stories told and truths uncovered.

In the realm of Arthurian legends, the search for truth amidst a tapestry of myths and embellishments is akin to unraveling a complex puzzle. **Comparative analysis** of different texts offers a systematic approach to discerning the core truths from the artistic liberties woven into these narratives. Historians and enthusiasts can create a clearer picture of the historical foundation behind these legendary tales by delving into various accounts of Excalibur's origin, Merlin's powers, and other pivotal elements.

Each Arthurian text carries the imprint of its author's intentions and cultural background, shaping the narrative in unique ways. **Diverse interpretations** emerge through these texts, reflecting the storytellers' perspectives and historical contexts. By examining these variations, we can gain insight into the motivations behind different portrayals of familiar characters and events, shedding light on the complexities of Arthurian lore.

Through **systematic comparison**, we can sift through the layers of myth and legend to distinguish between historical facts and imaginative embellishments. This process allows us to identify recurring themes and details across different texts, highlighting elements that may have roots in reality. We can construct a more accurate historical narrative of King Arthur and his legendary world by scrutinizing these textual nuances.

As we navigate the labyrinthine paths of Arthurian literature, it becomes evident that each text offers a unique perspective on familiar tales. **By juxtaposing** these accounts, we can uncover shared truths that withstand the test of time, transcending individual interpretations. This comparative approach enriches our understanding of Arthurian legends. It deepens our appreciation for the diverse tapestry of stories that have shaped our perception of this legendary era.

Unveiling the Layers: Dive Deeper into the Texts

In understanding the Arthurian legends, it is crucial to account for the diverse intentions and cultural backgrounds of the authors who shaped these tales. Each retelling of the Arthurian saga reflects the author's perspective and the societal norms and values prevalent during their time. **By delving into the backgrounds of these authors, we can unravel the layers of influence that have shaped our perceptions of Camelot, Excalibur, Merlin, and the Knights of the Round Table.**

Sir Thomas Malory, a fifteenth-century English writer, penned "Le Morte d'Arthur," a compilation of French and English Arthurian stories. Malory's work reflects the chivalric ideals of his time, emphasizing loyalty, honor, and courtly love. **His portrayal of King Arthur as a noble and just ruler resonates with the societal expectations of his era**, where notions of knighthood and honor held significant sway.

In contrast, **Geoffrey of Monmouth**, a twelfth-century Welsh cleric, introduced Merlin as a key figure in his writings on Arthurian legend. **Merlin's character in Geoffrey's works embodies Celtic mysticism and druidic influences**, reflecting a cultural connection to ancient pagan beliefs. Through Geoffrey's portrayal, we glimpse a blend of Christian and pagan elements that enrich the tapestry of Arthurian lore.

Moving forward, **Alfred Lord Tennyson**, a nineteenth-century poet laureate, crafted "Idylls of the King," infusing Victorian sensibilities into his retelling of the Arthurian mythos. **Tennyson's focus on themes like duty, morality, and social order mirrors the concerns of his era**, where industrialization and social change were reshaping British society.

Considering these different perspectives on Arthurian legend allows us to appreciate how **each author's unique background colors their portrayal** of characters and events. By recognizing this diversity in intent and cultural influence, we can better grasp the complexities of interpreting historical myths.

As we navigate through various Arthurian texts, it becomes evident that **the legends surrounding Camelot are not static but fluid,** evolving with each storyteller who adds their voice to the narrative. This dynamic nature underscores the richness of Arthurian lore while challenging us to discern between historical truths and artistic embellishments.

In our quest to uncover the essence of Camelot and its legendary inhabitants, **we must embrace the diversity of perspectives presented by different authors**. By acknowledging the varied intentions and cultural contexts that shape these narratives, we gain a deeper understanding of how myth and history intertwine to create enduring tales that captivate audiences across generations.

By examining these diverse portrayals with an open mind and critical eye, we can tease out **the threads of truth woven into the fabric of Arthurian legend**. By honoring the contributions of each author while dissecting their biases and influences, we inch closer to unraveling the mysteries surrounding Excalibur's origin, Merlin's powers, and the enigmatic realm of Camelot.

It is essential to approach the task with a critical and discerning eye when accessing methodologies for systematic comparison to establish a more accurate historical narrative. By delving into the various Arthurian texts with a keen focus on details and inconsistencies, we can unravel the layers of myth and legend to reveal the hidden historical truth. **Comparative analysis** is critical in this process, allowing us to sift through the divergent accounts and pinpoint common threads that may lead us closer to the reality behind the myths.

One effective method in this endeavor is to **examine the cultural backgrounds** of the authors who penned these Arthurian tales. Understanding their motivations, beliefs, and societal contexts can explain why certain aspects were embellished or altered in their narratives. By considering these influences, we can better discern between factual elements and artistic liberties woven into the stories of Excalibur and Merlin.

Moreover, **scrutinizing the intentions** behind each text is crucial in deciphering the truths they hold. Some authors may have aimed to glorify King Arthur as a legendary figure. In contrast, others might have sought to convey moral lessons or political allegories through their writings. By unraveling these underlying purposes, we can separate fact from fiction and create a more coherent historical narrative.

A **systematic approach** to comparison involves meticulous attention to detail and a methodical examination of each text's portrayal of vital Arthurian elements. By creating a framework for analysis that considers multiple versions of Excalibur's origin or Merlin's powers, we can identify patterns and discrepancies that may offer clues to their historical authenticity. This structured methodology allows us to navigate the maze of conflicting accounts with clarity and precision.

Through **rigorous research** and scholarly inquiry, we can sift through centuries of storytelling to unearth kernels of truth that have endured the test of time. By engaging with primary sources and historical documents alongside Arthurian legends, we can triangulate our findings and construct a more nuanced understanding of Camelot and its legendary inhabitants. This process requires patience, perseverance, and an unwavering commitment to uncovering the historical realities beneath the layers of myth.

In our quest for historical accuracy, we must **remain open-minded** and willing to challenge preconceived notions about King Arthur and his fabled realm. By embracing ambiguity and complexity in our analysis, we can cultivate a deeper appreciation for the multifaceted nature of Arthurian lore while honing our ability to precisely separate fact from fiction.

Ultimately, by accessing methodologies for systematic comparison, we equip ourselves with the tools necessary to untangle the web of Arthurian narratives and reconstruct a more authentic historical tapestry. Through diligent scholarship, critical thinking, and a passion for unraveling mysteries of the past, we embark on a journey toward a clearer understanding of Excalibur, Merlin, and the enduring legacy of Camelot.

Through the diligent process of comparative textual analysis, we have ventured deep into the heart of Arthurian legends, dissecting the intricate layers of narrative woven over centuries. This meticulous examination has illuminated the varied portrayals of Excalibur and Merlin and underscored the profound impact of cultural and authorial influences on these stories.

Core truths and artistic embellishments stand at the forefront of our exploration. We've unearthed a fascinating spectrum of interpretations and adaptations by comparing different Arthurian texts. Each version of the tale brings its own flavor, shaped by its author's times and personal inclinations. This diversity is not merely a testament to the adaptability of the legends but also serves as a rich canvas illustrating the evolution of storytelling itself.

Arthurian authors' **intentions and cultural backgrounds** play a crucial role in how these stories are told. Understanding the motives behind each author's choices offers us invaluable insights into each period's broader historical and social context. It's akin to peering through a window into the past, gaining a clearer view of the societal norms and values that influenced these narratives.

Our approach has been grounded in **systematic comparison**, a methodology that has enabled us to sift through the myths to catch glimpses of historical reality. This process is about finding discrepancies and appreciating the common threads that connect different accounts, helping us piece together a more coherent and plausible historical narrative.

As we move forward, let us carry the wisdom gleaned from this chapter. The legends of Excalibur and Merlin, enriched by centuries of storytelling, offer more than just entertainment; they mirror human nature and cultural identity. By embracing both the truths and the embellishments, we enrich our understanding of the past and the narrative arts that continue to shape our world.

Let this journey through the pages of history remind you of the power of inquiry and the importance of perspective. May it inspire you to question, explore, and appreciate the stories that have traveled through time to reach us, bearing the marks of countless minds and hands. Together, let us continue to unravel the mysteries of the past, armed with knowledge and fueled by curiosity.

Chapter 5: Demystifying Myths: Mastery of Research and Critical Thought

In the tranquil corners of the ancient library, Thomas shuffled through musty tomes and scattered papers under the dim glow of a solitary lamp. The weight of centuries seemed to press upon his shoulders as he searched for truths veiled by the shroud of legend. His fingers traced the spines of books that spoke of kings and knights, of chivalries long forgotten. Today, his quest was not for mere knowledge but for clarity—a delineation between myth and reality in the tales of King Arthur.

Outside, the world was veiled in twilight; shadows danced along cobblestone streets that had witnessed countless such pursuits. Inside, Thomas's mind wrestled with narratives woven by bards whose songs transcended time. He pondered on how these legends might hold kernels of historical truth. Was Excalibur real? Did Camelot exist? Each question pulled him deeper into an intellectual labyrinth.

From across the room, a draft stirred the pages of an open manuscript, snapping Thomas back from his reverie. He approached it cautiously as if it were a delicate relic capable of crumbling at a touch. The manuscript was a secondary source citing letters from medieval times—possibly letters penned by those who believed they had witnessed Arthur's reign. Here lay evidence that could bridge past with present, speculation with fact.

Thomas knew that understanding context was crucial; biases in these accounts could skew interpretations and lead history astray. He sifted through each document meticulously, discerning authorial intent and cross-referencing facts where possible. This was not merely academic rigor but a personal journey to peel back layers of lore to reveal history's true face.

As he absorbed himself in this task, night deepened around him. The library became a sanctuary where time stood still—each tick of the clock measured not seconds but revelations.

Why do we cling to legends like those of Arthur and his knights? What do they say about us as seekers of truth in our own right?

Peeling Back the Layers of Legend: How Do We Discern Truth from Myth?

The allure of Arthurian legends has captivated the minds and hearts of scholars, historians, and enthusiasts for centuries. The stories of Merlin's wisdom and Excalibur's might are more than just tales; they are woven into the fabric of cultural history. But how much of what we know is steeped in myth, and what truths lie beneath? This chapter will equip you with the tools to separate fact from fiction using robust research methodologies and critical thought processes.

The journey into the heart of these legends requires more than cursive reading; it demands a meticulous approach to distinguishing historical fact from embellished narrative. The essence of this exploration lies not in disproving the magic of these tales but in enriching our understanding by uncovering their historical underpinnings. By applying **critical analysis**, we can sift through centuries of storytelling to identify kernels of truth that have survived the embellishments of time.

In our quest for clarity, we will explore advanced research techniques designed to unearth reliable sources that shed light on the murky waters of legend. These techniques are not just tools; they are keys that unlock doors to past worlds, offering insights that challenge our preconceptions. It's about asking the right questions and having the tenacity to pursue those answers, even when they lead us down unexpected paths.

Furthermore, effectively utilizing primary and secondary sources is crucial in constructing a factual discussion around these age-old stories. Primary sources give us direct snapshots of history untainted by modern interpretations. In contrast, secondary sources offer scholarly perspectives that can either challenge or support our findings. The interplay between these sources will guide us in painting a more accurate picture of Arthurian times.

This exploration is not merely academic; it's a journey that connects us with the thinkers, writers, and leaders of yesteryears. Each piece of evidence we gather and each source we scrutinize adds layers to our understanding of Merlin and Excalibur, transforming them from mythical figures into historical entities with stories rooted in actual events and natural contexts.

As we navigate through this chapter, remember that our goal is not just to learn about methods but to apply them in ways that breathe new life into old legends. We're on a quest not merely to understand what to think but how to think about the lore surrounding Excalibur and Merlin. This approach doesn't diminish the magic but enhances our appreciation by connecting us more deeply with the past.

Join me as we embark on this enlightening journey to bridge the gap between myth and reality, armed with critical thought and rigorous research methodologies. Together, let's uncover the layers of history veiled beneath centuries-old narratives and discover where fact meets folklore in the legendary tales of King Arthur's court.

Researching Arthurian legends requires a keen eye for separating fact from fiction. The allure of myths often obscures historical truths, making it essential to apply critical analysis to unravel the complex tapestry of legends surrounding figures like King Arthur and Merlin. By delving deep into the narratives, one can sift through the layers of embellishment to uncover the nuggets of reality at their core. **Critical**

analysis is a torch in the darkness of myth, illuminating the path toward historical accuracy.

In the realm of Arthurian legends, separating myth from reality is akin to unraveling a tangled knot. Each story passed down through generations carries elements of imagination and exaggeration that blur the lines between truth and fantasy. **Researchers can untangle these threads through critical analysis, discerning the historical realities that underpin even the most fantastical tales.** Questioning the narratives' motives, biases, and inconsistencies can create a clearer picture of the past.

Unraveling myths requires a willingness to challenge preconceived notions and popular beliefs. **It demands a sharp intellect and a discerning eye**, capable of distinguishing between embellishments added for entertainment value and authentic historical details. By scrutinizing each account critically, researchers can separate the wheat from the chaff, identifying reliable sources and discarding dubious claims.

Moreover, critical analysis invites researchers to explore beyond the surface of the stories, delving into the cultural and social contexts in which they were crafted. **Understanding the motivations behind the creation of these myths** sheds light on why specific details were exaggerated or altered over time. By placing each narrative within its historical framework, researchers can glean valuable insights into the values and beliefs of past societies.

As we navigate through the labyrinthine world of Arthurian legends, armed with critical analysis as our guide, we begin to unravel the intricate web of myths that have shrouded historical truths for centuries. **By peeling back layers of storytelling and interpretation,** we reveal glimpses of a past obscured by time and embellishment. Through careful examination and thoughtful reflection, we pave the way for a deeper understanding of the legendary figures that continue to captivate our imaginations.

Continue your journey into unraveling historical myths by exploring advanced research techniques in sourcing reliable information.

Implementing advanced research techniques is crucial in unraveling the mysteries surrounding historical myths, particularly Arthurian legends. To navigate the intricate web of stories and separate fact from fiction, researchers must hone their skills in sourcing reliable information. By delving deep into primary and secondary sources, a clearer picture of the historical context can emerge, shedding light on the truths behind the myths.

One key aspect of advanced research techniques is the ability to discern between credible and dubious sources. In the age of information overload, distinguishing reliable sources from unreliable ones is paramount. Researchers must be vigilant in evaluating their sources' authority, expertise, and biases to ensure their findings' accuracy and validity. By employing critical thinking and discernment, scholars can sift through the vast sea of information to uncover hidden gems of truth.

Engaging with primary sources is another essential component of advanced research techniques. Primary sources provide firsthand accounts or direct evidence of historical events, offering invaluable insights into the past. By immersing oneself in original documents, artifacts, or recordings, researchers can access unfiltered information that forms the foundation of scholarly inquiry. The meticulous examination of primary sources allows for a more nuanced understanding of historical narratives, enabling researchers to piece together a more accurate depiction of events.

Furthermore, leveraging secondary sources complements the exploration of primary materials. Secondary sources offer interpretations, analyses, and critiques of primary data, enriching the research process with diverse perspectives and scholarly discourse. By engaging with a range of secondary materials, such as academic articles, books, and essays, researchers can contextualize their findings within broader scholarly conversations. This multifaceted approach enhances the depth and breadth of research inquiries, fostering a more comprehensive understanding of complex historical phenomena.

Advanced research techniques also involve employing innovative methodologies to uncover hidden truths. From digital humanities tools to interdisciplinary approaches, researchers can harness various methods to illuminate obscured facets of historical myths. By thinking creatively and embracing cutting-edge technologies, scholars can transcend conventional boundaries and delve deeper into the intricacies of Arthurian legends. This spirit of innovation enriches research endeavors and inspires new avenues for exploration and discovery.

In conclusion, mastering advanced research techniques is essential for demystifying historical myths embedded within Arthurian legends. By honing critical analysis skills, engaging effectively with primary and secondary sources, and adopting innovative methodologies, researchers can unravel the complexities of these ancient narratives with precision and clarity. A more authentic understanding of Arthurian legends can be achieved through diligent scholarship and unwavering dedication to truth-seeking.

Research Framework: Source Evaluation and Synthesis

This research framework is designed to guide scholars and enthusiasts in effectively utilizing primary and secondary sources to construct factual discussions about Arthurian legends. By following a structured approach, researchers can navigate the vast landscape of historical narratives with precision and critical understanding.

Identification and Collection of Sources

The first step in this framework is **identifying relevant** primary and secondary sources. The research topic is crucial to gathering credible, reliable, and pertinent materials. This involves scouring libraries, digital archives, academic databases, and scholarly journals to compile various resources.

Credibility Assessment

Once sources have been identified, the next phase involves **evaluating** their credibility. Researchers must scrutinize each source for biases, inaccuracies, and relevance to ensure that only trustworthy information forms the basis of their discussions. Scholars can construct well-informed arguments by discerning between fact and fiction within the texts.

Utilization of Databases and Scholarly Journals

Utilizing **databases and scholarly journals** is essential to enhance the depth of research. These platforms offer a wealth of academic knowledge that can provide nuanced insights into Arthurian literature. Researchers should leverage these resources to access cutting-edge scholarship and diverse perspectives on the subject matter.

NOTE-TAKING METHODOLOGIES

Effective **note-taking** strategies play a pivotal role in synthesizing information from various sources. Researchers should adopt organized methods for recording key points, quotations, and references to facilitate the later synthesis. Scholars can create cohesive narratives from disparate sources by categorizing notes thematically and chronologically.

Synthesizing Information

The final stage of this framework involves **synthesizing information** gathered from primary and secondary sources. Researchers can draw connections between texts by employing thematic analysis and comparative studies, identifying patterns, and extracting overarching themes from the data. This synthesis forms the backbone of constructing factual discussions rooted in historical accuracy.

Practical Implications

By adhering to this research framework, scholars can construct well-founded arguments distinguishing myth and reality in Arthurian literature. This structured approach ensures the credibility of the research. It empowers researchers to delve deeper into historical narratives with clarity and precision.

Future Development

As research methodologies evolve, this framework must adapt to incorporate new technologies, sources, and analytical tools. By staying abreast of advancements in the field of Arthurian studies, researchers can refine their approaches to sourcing, evaluating, and synthesizing information effectively. The continuous development of this framework ensures that scholars remain at the forefront of demystifying historical myths surrounding Arthurian legends.

Navigating the Labyrinth: A Methodical Approach to Arthurian Realities

Mastering the delicate art of separating fact from fiction in Arthurian legends necessitates a structured approach, blending rigorous research with keen critical analysis. This chapter has laid a solid foundation, guiding you through the essential steps to elevate your understanding and appreciation of these historical and mythical narratives. Here's how you can apply these strategies in a systematic, engaging, and effective manner.

Step 1: Developing Critical Analysis Skills

Start by honing your ability to question and critique. Engage with diverse Arthurian sources—texts, films, or artworks—and challenge their authenticity and biases. This skill will empower you to discern historical truths from embellished tales, enhancing your knowledge and analytical prowess.

Step 2: Implementing Advanced Research Techniques

Expand your research beyond superficial layers by diving into academic databases and historical archives. This deeper investigative approach will uncover more nuanced insights and reliable information, crucial for constructing a well-rounded perspective on Arthurian legends.

STEP 3: UTILIZING PRIMARY and Secondary Sources

Embrace the rich tapestry of primary sources available, from medieval manuscripts to early modern interpretations. Complement these with secondary analyses to broaden your understanding. This balanced sourcing is essential for crafting informed and credible discussions about the legends.

Step 4: Constructing Factual Discussions

With a wealth of information, focus on articulating your findings clearly and logically. Synthesize data from various sources to build solid and evidence-backed arguments. This step is vital in sharing your insights with others and contributing to the scholarly dialogue on Arthurian myths.

Step 5: Balancing Factual Accuracy and Artistic Interpretation

Finally, recognize the interplay between historical accuracy and artistic expression. Appreciate the creative renditions of Arthurian tales while grounding your interpretations in factual evidence. This balance will enrich your understanding and allow you to appreciate the legends in both historical and cultural contexts.

By following these steps, you enrich your knowledge and contribute to the ongoing exploration of one of the most captivating legends in history. Each step is designed to build upon the last, ensuring a comprehensive mastery of the material. Remember, the journey through Arthurian lore is as rewarding as it is enlightening, filled with discoveries that bridge the past with the present.

This systematic approach serves as a tool for academic exploration and a means to foster a deeper appreciation for the art of storytelling through history. By critically engaging with the legends of Arthur, Merlin, and Excalibur, you become part of a centuries-old tradition of inquiry and discourse. Embrace this journey with curiosity and rigor, and let the true story of these legendary figures unfold before you.

Chapter 6: Scholars of the Round Table: Engaging with the Academic Community

In the dimly lit confines of a quaint library nestled in a small town steeped in history, Eleanor sat absorbed by the weight of ancient texts surrounding her. Her eyes danced across the page of a particularly well-worn book on Arthurian legends, the musty scent of old paper mingling with the faint aroma of rain seeping through the open window. The soft pitter-patter offered a rhythmic backdrop to her concentrated study.

Outside, the world moved slowly. Leaves whispered secrets to each other as they fluttered in the gentle breeze, and a church bell tolled with melancholic regularity somewhere in the distance. Eleanor's mind raced through centuries of lore and scholarly debate, connecting dots many had overlooked. She was preparing for an upcoming medieval conference, where she aimed to present her findings on lesser-known influences on Arthurian tales.

Her research wasn't just academic; it was personal. Her grandfather had been a historian with an enchanting knack for storytelling, weaving tales of knights and chivalry that had shaped her childhood. Now gone, his memory fueled her pursuit for deeper understanding and novel interpretations. As she flipped through another page, a note slipped out—a scribble in her grandfather's familiar hand pointing out an obscure reference to a Celtic deity thought to influence Merlin's character.

This discovery sparked excitement but also doubt. Was she seeing connections where there were none? The academic community could be fiercely critical, and the fear of presenting unfounded theories gnawed at her confidence. Yet, this was her chance to contribute something meaningful, to add layers to the collective understanding of these ancient stories.

She paused, leaned back in her chair, and stared at the greying sky as students passed outside, lost in their own worlds. Their laughter brought her back from medieval realms to present realities. She pondered how sharing these insights at forums could challenge existing narratives and inspire others like herself who sought truth in tales long told.

As evening crept over the horizon, painting it with strokes of orange and pink, Eleanor gathered her notes and prepared to leave. The quiet comfort of the library had always been her sanctuary—a place where the past met the present, and ideas flowed freely.

As she stepped out into the fresh air, still thinking about Arthurian legends—their mysteries wrapped within layers of history—she wondered: How might uncovering new aspects of these stories change our view of history?

Unraveling the Threads of Legend: Why Scholarly Engagement Matters

Engaging with the academic community is not merely a formal exercise but a vital step toward deepening our understanding of the complex tapestry that makes up Arthurian legends. As we delve into the realm of King Arthur, Excalibur, and Merlin, it becomes increasingly clear that to truly appreciate these stories, one must venture beyond the surface and explore the myriad interpretations and scholarly debates surrounding them.

The essence of this exploration lies in participating in academic forums and conferences focused on medieval or mythological studies. These gatherings are not just congregations of experts; they are vibrant hubs of knowledge where ideas are exchanged freely and theories are formed and challenged. **The benefit of such participation** is manifold, offering fresh perspectives and insights that may remain uncovered in solitary study. This collaborative environment fosters a deeper understanding and appreciation of the nuances in Arthurian lore, highlighting the importance of community in the pursuit of knowledge.

Moreover, **sharing insights and engaging in debates within** these scholarly communities does more than broaden individual understanding—it enriches the entire field. As researchers and enthusiasts dissect and discuss their interpretations and findings, they contribute to a living, evolving narrative. This dynamic discourse helps challenge prevailing myths and misconceptions about these legends, paving the way for a more nuanced comprehension informed by diverse viewpoints.

Collaborative opportunities within these academic circles are also crucial. They allow for resource pooling, sharing unique research materials, and joint ventures in exploring uncharted aspects of the Arthurian legends. Such collaborations can lead to groundbreaking discoveries that might be difficult to achieve through individual efforts alone. Identifying these opportunities is essential for anyone seriously contributing to the Arthurian lore discourse.

Reflecting on personal experiences with these scholarly platforms reveals their transformative potential. Engaging with other academics at conferences or contributing to forums has expanded my understanding and connected me with like-minded individuals passionate about medieval history and mythology. These connections often lead to fruitful collaborations and continuous learning opportunities that extend well beyond the confines of any single event or discussion.

As we navigate this chapter, we will explore how these scholarly interactions enhance our comprehension and invigorate our passion for uncovering the layers beneath the legends of King Arthur. The journey through academic engagement is as rewarding as it is enlightening, offering pathways to not only master but also contribute to the lore we so cherish.

By embracing these scholarly communities, we open ourselves up to a world where every debate enriches our knowledge, every conference sparks new ideas, and every collaboration brings us closer to unraveling the truths hidden within centuries-old myths. This engagement is not just about learning—it's about actively participating in preserving and evolving cultural heritage that fascinates us today.

Participating in academic forums and conferences focused on medieval or mythological studies can benefit those seeking a deeper understanding of Arthurian lore. These platforms offer unique opportunities to engage with scholars, researchers, and enthusiasts who share a passion for unraveling the mysteries and truths behind the legends of King Arthur, Excalibur, and Merlin. By immersing oneself in these academic circles, individuals can access a wealth of knowledge, diverse perspectives, and cutting-edge research that can enrich their comprehension of the historical and cultural contexts surrounding Arthurian tales.

Attending conferences allows individuals to *immerse themselves in a stimulating environment* where ideas are exchanged, debates are sparked, and new insights are revealed. Engaging in discussions with experts in the field can *deepen one's understanding* of the complexities inherent in Arthurian legends, shedding light on obscure references, historical inaccuracies, and cultural nuances that may have been overlooked. Furthermore, these interactions can *challenge preconceived notions* and encourage critical thinking, prompting attendees to question popular misconceptions and delve into the layers of truth hidden within the narratives.

One key benefit of participating in academic forums is the *opportunity for networking*. Building connections with like-minded individuals passionate about medieval studies can open doors to collaborative projects, research opportunities, and mentorship relationships. Through these connections, individuals can expand their knowledge base, receive feedback on their own research or interpretations, and potentially contribute to advancing scholarship in Arthurian studies.

Conferences also provide a platform for individuals to *present their research*, theories, or analyses related to Arthurian legends. This allows them to receive valuable feedback from peers and actively contribute to the academic discourse surrounding these timeless tales. By sharing their insights with a knowledgeable audience, individuals can refine their arguments, strengthen their positions, and influence future research directions within the field.

Moreover, engaging with scholarly communities through conferences and forums can *inspire individuals* to pursue further studies or research endeavors related to Arthurian lore. The passion and dedication exhibited by fellow academics and enthusiasts can ignite a spark of curiosity and motivation in attendees, encouraging them to explore new avenues of inquiry or embark on ambitious projects that deepen our collective understanding of these legendary stories.

Continue reading about how sharing insights within scholarly communities enhances understanding of Arthurian lore.

Engaging with scholarly communities enhances our understanding of Arthurian lore by fostering a space for sharing insights and debates that deepen our comprehension of these ancient tales. **Within academic circles, the exchange of knowledge and critical discussions can shed light on different interpretations, historical contexts, and cultural significance embedded in Arthurian legends**. By participating in these conversations, enthusiasts can glean new perspectives, challenge existing beliefs, and broaden their understanding of the complexities within these stories.

Sharing insights within scholarly communities allows for a rich tapestry of perspectives to emerge, weaving together various viewpoints to create a nuanced understanding of Arthurian lore. Through these interactions, individuals can uncover hidden meanings, analyze characters' motivations, and explore the moral dilemmas presented in these timeless tales. *These discussions provide a platform for collective learning and growth, where each participant contributes a unique piece to the puzzle of unraveling the mysteries surrounding King Arthur and his knights.*

In academic forums dedicated to medieval or mythological studies, **debates catalyze intellectual growth**, pushing participants to question assumptions, reevaluate interpretations, and delve deeper into the layers of Arthurian legends. *These debates challenge preconceived notions and encourage individuals to think critically and engage with the material more profoundly.* By actively participating in these discussions, individuals can refine their analytical skills, enhance their research abilities, and develop a more nuanced perspective on the intricate web of stories that make up the Arthurian mythos.

Sharing insights within scholarly communities can spark creativity and inspire new avenues of exploration. Through collaborative engagements with fellow enthusiasts and academics, individuals can uncover connections between different versions of Arthurian tales, draw parallels with other mythologies, and even propose fresh interpretations that breathe new life into these age-old narratives. *By immersing oneself in these conversations and debates, one opens up a world of possibilities for reinterpretation and reinvention within the realm of Arthurian lore.*

Ultimately, engaging with academic communities provides a platform for continuous learning and growth, allowing individuals to deepen their appreciation for the richness and complexity of Arthurian legends. *By actively participating in these scholarly discussions, enthusiasts can embark on a journey of discovery that transcends mere* *storytelling*, delving into the heart of cultural heritage, historical truths, and enduring themes that resonate across generations.

Collaborating with the academic community offers many opportunities to delve deeper into the rich tapestry of Arthurian legends. **By engaging with scholars, enthusiasts can contribute to the ongoing discourse surrounding these timeless tales.** One way to partake in this academic exchange is through collaborative research projects. **Individuals can bring fresh perspectives and insights by teaming up with scholars and researchers.** This collaboration enriches one's own understanding and adds valuable contributions to the collective knowledge pool on Arthurian lore.

Academic conferences dedicated to medieval or mythological studies are another avenue for those eager to engage in scholarly discussions. These gatherings provide platforms for individuals to share their interpretations, findings, and theories with like-minded individuals equally passionate about unraveling the mysteries of Arthurian legends. **By attending these conferences, enthusiasts can network with experts in the field, exchange ideas, and gain new perspectives that can shape their understanding of these ancient tales.**

Moreover, **joining societies or organizations focused on medieval literature or mythology offers a more structured approach to contributing to the academic discourse on Arthurian legends.** These communities often host regular events, publish journals, and foster collaborations among members. **By becoming an active member of such groups, individuals can immerse themselves in scholarly debates, access valuable resources, and publish their own research or articles related to Arthurian studies.**

Another collaborative opportunity is contributing to academic publications and journals dedicated to Arthurian studies. By submitting articles or papers for publication, enthusiasts can share their insights with a broader audience within the educational community.

This allows for personal growth and recognition and aids in advancing the collective understanding of Arthurian legends by introducing new perspectives and interpretations into the scholarly conversation.

Furthermore, **engaging with online forums and discussion groups focused on medieval literature or mythology can be convenient for connecting with fellow enthusiasts and scholars worldwide**. These virtual spaces provide:

- Platforms for sharing ideas.
- Seeking feedback on research findings.
- Engaging in lively debates on various aspects of Arthurian lore.

By actively participating in these online communities, individuals can stay updated on the latest research trends, exchange knowledge, and build meaningful connections within the academic realm.

In essence, **collaborative opportunities within the academic community present a gateway for individuals to deepen their understanding of Arthurian legends while actively contributing to the ongoing scholarly conversation**. Whether through research projects, conference participation, society memberships, publication submissions, or online engagements, each avenue offers a unique way for enthusiasts to immerse themselves in medieval literature and mythology. **By seizing these collaborative opportunities**, individuals can play a vital role in shaping the future narratives surrounding Arthurian lore and perpetuating its enduring legacy for generations.

Engaging with the academic community through forums and conferences is beneficial; it is crucial for anyone sincerely interested in unraveling the complexities of Arthurian lore. These interactions serve as a vibrant conduit for exchanging ideas, fostering a collaborative environment where scholars and enthusiasts can challenge and refine their understanding of the legends.

Participation in these academic gatherings allows us to step beyond the confines of solitary study, immersing ourselves in a dynamic dialogue with others who share our passion. This collective exploration enriches our perspectives, making us privy to diverse interpretations and lesser-known aspects of medieval narratives. The robust debates and discussions that characterize such forums are instrumental in pushing the boundaries of what we know and understand about the Arthurian age.

Moreover, the collaborative opportunities available in these settings are invaluable. Working together on papers, panels, or research projects, we can contribute to a larger body of knowledge, ensuring that the richness of Arthurian legends continues to inspire and educate future generations. Through these partnerships, we can challenge outdated myths and breathe new life into the historical and cultural layers of these enduring tales.

Reflecting on engaging with the academic community, it becomes clear that this is not merely an academic exercise but a journey of continual discovery and personal growth. The insights gained and the relationships forged in these scholarly circles resonate far beyond the conference rooms and lecture halls, influencing our narratives and approaches to the lore.

Let us approach each opportunity for collaboration with openness and enthusiasm, eager to share and grow. Through these scholarly engagements, we not only deepen our understanding but also ensure that the enchanting world of King Arthur and his Knights remains a vibrant field of study, rich with scholarly intrigue and ripe for future exploration.

Fostering these academic connections does more than

expand our intellectual horizons. We become active participants in the living history of Arthurian studies, contributing to a legacy of knowledge that transcends time and place. Let this motivate us to continue reaching out, engaging, and innovating within this fascinating field.

Chapter 7: From Pages to Pop Culture: The Modern Influence of Ancient Myths

Professor Eleanor Davies stood by her study window in the quiet of an early morning in a small Welsh village, where the mist clung to the rolling hills like a lingering whisper. Her eyes traced the ancient outline of the distant castle ruins, remnants of legends carved into stone and grass. Today, she was to lecture on Arthurian myths at the local university—a topic that filled her life with passion and turmoil.

Eleanor's mind wandered back to her childhood days spent listening to her grandfather recount tales of King Arthur and his knights. Those stories shaped her and guided her academic career. Yet now, as she prepared for her lecture, she felt a twinge of uncertainty. How much did these ancient myths still resonate in a vastly changed world?

Her thoughts were interrupted by the soft sound of footsteps on the wooden floor behind her. Her husband, Rhys, approached with a gentle smile. "You're lost in thought again," he observed.

"Just reflecting on how these stories have evolved," Eleanor replied, turning from the window to face him. The room around them was filled with books and papers scattered across every surface—a testament to Eleanor's relentless pursuit of knowledge.

Rhys nodded thoughtfully. "And how do they continue to shape our culture today?"

"Exactly." She sighed lightly. The weight of responsibility pressed upon her, not just to teach but to highlight how each retelling of these myths through films, books, and other media reshaped society's values and perceptions.

Later that day at the university, Eleanor stood before a room filled with eager faces. She noticed varied student reactions as she spoke about contemporary adaptations—from blockbuster movies like "Excalibur" to modern novels reimagining Merlin's magic. Some seemed captivated, while others appeared skeptical.

"Consider this," Eleanor proposed during the discussion segment of her lecture, "How might understanding Merlin's character development or Excalibur's symbolism influence not only our appreciation of these tales but also our broader cultural ethos?"

The question lingered in the air as students debated among themselves; some argued that these were mere stories with no real impact on modern values, while others countered vehemently about their deep cultural significance.

Eleanor ambled towards home as dusk fell and shadows stretched across campus paths lined by old oaks and modern sculptures. She pondered her students' passionate and indifferent responses and wondered about the future relevance of these ancient narratives.

Had Arthurian legends indeed adapted enough to remain meaningful in this high-tech age? Or were they destined to become nothing more than relics studied by academics like herself? As she crossed an old stone bridge that arched over a quietly babbling brook near her home, she mused: Are we shaping these stories, or are they still shaping us?

Unraveling the Threads of Time: How Arthurian Myths Shape Our Modern World

The tales of King Arthur, Excalibur, and the enigmatic Merlin have long captivated audiences, transcending the boundaries of mere folklore to become foundational elements in modern culture. This chapter explores the historical and literary significance of these legends and their profound influence on contemporary media and societal values. We can uncover how ancient narratives continue to shape and inspire our world by delving into how these age-old stories are reimagined today.

With its rich tapestry of chivalry, magic, and heroism, Arthurian mythology provides fertile ground for countless adaptations. From blockbuster films to bestselling novels, these stories have been reshaped to suit the tastes and sensibilities of modern audiences. However, this transformation is not merely aesthetic; it has more profound implications for how we perceive history, morality, and even our identities. Through a detailed examination of these adaptations, this chapter aims to reveal how ancient myths are not static relics but dynamic elements that contribute to ongoing cultural conversations.

The Journey from Medieval Pages to Modern Screens

One must recognize the visual spectacle and narrative depth that contemporary cinema and literature bring to Arthurian legends. These adaptations often reflect current social norms and issues, influencing public perception subtly yet significantly. For instance, the portrayal of Merlin as a wise but flawed wizard in recent films contrasts sharply with his more detached and mysterious depiction in early texts. This shift invites viewers to reflect more nuancedly on the complexity of wisdom and power.

Moreover, Excalibur's evolution from a symbol of divine kingship to a beacon of personal empowerment highlights how cultural values have shifted toward individualism and self-realization. By analyzing these thematic shifts, we gain insights into these myths' timeless appeal and capacity to adapt to contemporary values.

Academia's Role in Myth-Making

The influence of scholarly work on popular interpretations of Arthurian tales is profound. Academic research does not just reside in journals and conferences; it trickles down into novels, movies, television shows, and even video games, shaping their narratives fundamentally. This chapter will explore how academic debates about Merlin's historical authenticity or Excalibur's symbolic meanings inform their portrayal in popular culture. Understanding this relationship between academia and media is crucial for appreciating how deeply interconnected our entertainment is with historical scholarship.

By exploring these various facets, we can appreciate the full spectrum of Arthurian mythology's role in modern culture—the adaptation process in media, the impact on societal norms and values, and the academic underpinnings that guide these portrayals. Each adaptation mirrors our collective aspirations, fears, and values through the lens of ancient heroes' tales.

By engaging with these stories thoughtfully and critically, we enjoy a richer entertainment experience and participate more fully in the ongoing dialogue about who we are as a society. This chapter invites readers to join this exploration, offering a deeper understanding of cultural dynamics and a renewed appreciation for how ancient stories can illuminate modern life's complexities.

In essence, by tracing how Excalibur cuts through the fabric of time or how Merlin's wisdom echoes through ages into our present-day consciousness, we connect more profoundly with past legends and our current reality. As we progress through this chapter, let us keep an open mind about how much our perceptions are shaped by these age-old narratives that continue to enchant us today.

The adaptation of Arthurian myths has been a prevalent and enduring trend in modern literature, movies, and various media forms. These ancient stories have transcended time, captivating audiences with their tales of chivalry, magic, and destiny. From the sword Excalibur to the wizard Merlin, these legendary figures have become iconic symbols in popular culture, shaping how we perceive heroism and adventure.

Arthurian legends have been reimagined in countless ways, from classic novels like T.H. White's "The Once and Future King" to blockbuster films such as "Excalibur" and "King Arthur." Each adaptation brings a fresh perspective to the age-old stories, breathing new life into characters that have stood the test of time. The allure of Camelot and the Knights of the Round Table continues to inspire storytellers and audiences alike, showcasing the timeless appeal of these mythical narratives.

In contemporary literature, authors often draw upon **Arthurian myths** as inspiration, infusing their unique twists and interpretations into familiar tales. By reinterpreting these ancient stories through a modern lens, writers can explore themes of power, love, betrayal, and redemption in ways that resonate with today's readers. This fusion of old and new creates a rich tapestry of storytelling that bridges the gap between past and present.

Similarly, filmmakers have capitalized on the enduring popularity of **Arthurian legends** in movies and television shows by bringing them to life on the big screen. Whether through epic fantasy films or gritty historical dramas, directors have showcased the fantastical elements of Camelot alongside the complex characters that inhabit this mythical world. By visually depicting the grandeur and tragedy of Arthur's court, filmmakers can transport audiences to a time long gone while exploring universal themes that still hold relevance today.

Dive deeper into how these adaptations influence our modern society's public perceptions and cultural values.

Analyzing the implications of modern adaptations of Arthurian myths on public perceptions and cultural values reveals that these stories hold significant power in shaping contemporary beliefs and attitudes. *The retelling of these ancient legends in various forms of media, such as literature, movies, and television shows, influences how audiences perceive medieval history and its associated values.* When filmmakers or authors reinterpret characters like King Arthur, Merlin, or Guinevere, they imbue them with qualities that reflect current societal norms and ideals.

One crucial impact of these adaptations is the perpetuation of certain stereotypes or misconceptions about the medieval era. By portraying knights as chivalrous saviors or damsels in distress awaiting rescue, media representations can reinforce gender norms that may not accurately reflect the complexities of historical relationships. *These simplified portrayals risk oversimplifying the rich tapestry of medieval life and perpetuate outdated notions about gender roles.*

Moreover, *how magic and supernatural elements are depicted in modern adaptations can influence beliefs about spirituality and the unknown.* The portrayal of Merlin as a wise wizard or Excalibur as a mystical sword can shape viewers' perceptions of what is possible beyond the realm of science. *These adaptations blur the lines between myth and reality, inviting audiences to consider the existence of forces beyond our understanding.*

Cultural values are also deeply intertwined with how Arthurian myths are adapted for contemporary audiences. These stories' emphasis on honor, loyalty, and sacrifice resonates with timeless themes that remain relevant today. Modern adaptations reinforce the importance of integrity and courage in the face of adversity by showcasing characters who uphold these virtues.

In a world filled with uncertainty and rapid change, *the enduring popularity of Arthurian myths offers a sense of continuity and connection to our past.* These stories remind us of our shared human experiences across generations and cultures, highlighting universal love, betrayal, and redemption themes. *By exploring these timeless narratives through modern adaptations, audiences can find solace in the enduring power of storytelling to illuminate truths about the human condition.*

As we navigate the complexities of contemporary society, *the lessons embedded within Arthurian myths serve as guiding beacons, offering insights into leadership, friendship, and personal growth.* Analyzing how these stories are reimagined for new audiences allows us to gain a deeper understanding not only of our past but also of ourselves. *The impact of these adaptations on public perceptions underscores the enduring relevance of mythology in shaping cultural values and societal norms.*

Understanding how academia influences the portrayal of Arthurian myths in modern cultural expressions reveals that the scholarly examination of these legends shapes the way they are interpreted and represented in various media. **Academic research provides a foundation of knowledge** that creators draw upon when adapting these stories, ensuring historical accuracy and depth in their retellings. By delving into the original texts and historical contexts, scholars offer valuable insights into the themes, characters, and symbolism of Arthurian myths.

One significant influence of academia on modern adaptations is the emphasis on authenticity. Scholars strive to uncover the historical truths behind these myths, separating fact from fiction to present a more accurate portrayal of Arthurian legends. This commitment to authenticity seeps into contemporary interpretations, enriching them with credibility and depth that resonates with audiences seeking a deeper understanding of these timeless tales.

Moreover, academia contributes to the nuanced portrayal of characters and themes within Arthurian myths. By analyzing the complexities of figures like King Arthur, Merlin, and Guinevere, scholars offer interpretations beyond surface-level portrayals, providing a richer tapestry from which modern adaptations can be drawn. This depth of character development adds layers of meaning to contemporary retellings, allowing for more intricate and compelling storytelling.

Academic research also illuminates the cultural significance of Arthurian myths, showcasing how these stories have evolved over time and been influenced by various historical and societal factors. By exploring the origins and evolution of these legends, scholars offer valuable context that informs modern adaptations, ensuring that they resonate with contemporary audiences while staying true to the essence of the original tales.

Furthermore, academia is a guiding force in maintaining the integrity of Arthurian myths in modern cultural expressions. By upholding academic standards of research and analysis, scholars help creators navigate the vast landscape of Arthurian lore, steering them away from misinterpretations or misrepresentations that could distort the essence of these timeless stories. This dedication to preserving the authenticity and integrity of Arthurian myths ensures that their legacy continues to captivate audiences for generations.

In conclusion, **academia's influence on modern adaptations of Arthurian myths is profound**. By providing a foundation of knowledge, emphasizing authenticity, delving into character complexities, exploring cultural significance, and maintaining integrity, scholars play a crucial role in shaping how these timeless tales are portrayed in contemporary literature, movies, and other forms of pop culture. Their dedication to uncovering truths and presenting nuanced interpretations enriches our understanding of Arthurian legends. It ensures that their magic endures through the ages.

The enduring resonance of Arthurian legends in modern culture is a testament to their timeless appeal. It highlights these ancient stories' profound impact on contemporary societal values and perceptions. The journey through literature, film, and academia reveals that these narratives are more than just relics of the past; they are vibrant, evolving scripts that continue to shape and reflect the ethos of our times.

Understanding the adaptation of Arthurian myths in today's media is crucial. It shows us how the themes of chivalry, honor, and destiny resonate with and inspire current generations. Each reinterpretation, whether through a novel or a screenplay, is not only an homage to these age-old tales but also a mirror reflecting modern-day dilemmas and cultural dynamics. This interplay between the old and the new enriches our understanding and appreciation of the legends and our contemporary world.

The **implications of these adaptations on public perceptions** cannot be overstated. When filmmakers and authors infuse contemporary issues into the framework of ancient myths, they create a powerful platform for dialogue and reflection. For instance, the portrayal of Merlin's wisdom or Excalibur's symbolism in modern struggles for power or integrity brings these concepts closer to home, making them more relevant and impactful.

Furthermore, the role of **academia in influencing the portrayal** of these stories underscores the responsibility of scholars and educators in shaping cultural narratives. Their insights and analyses help ensure that adaptations remain faithful to the original myths' spirit while resonating with current audiences. This scholarly influence ensures a balanced perspective that honors the past while embracing the present.

As we move forward, let us remember that these stories are not static; they are dynamic narratives that continue to evolve with us. They offer a unique lens through which to view our world and understand our place within it. By engaging with these legends, we preserve their legacy and enrich our cultural dialogue and personal growth.

Let this exploration remind us of the power of storytelling in bridging worlds and generations. May it inspire us to delve deeper into our cultural heritage and discover the timeless wisdom embedded in these ancient narratives. The journey through Arthurian legends is a vivid illustration of how the past can inform and elevate the present, guiding us through the complexities of modern life with lessons that are as relevant today as they were centuries ago.

Chapter 8: Through the Looking Glass: Exploring Textual Diversity in Arthurian Legends

In the gentle embrace of twilight, the village of Elden rested under a sky painted with the soft hues of an ending day. The cool and crisp air whispered through the leaves of ancient oaks that stood as silent sentinaries around the modest stone church at its heart. Here, Eleanor sat on a worn wooden bench, her eyes tracing the veins of a fallen leaf she had picked up. Her thoughts were distant, echoing with tales of Arthurian legend—of Excalibur and Merlin—that her grandfather had told her under these very trees.

Eleanor was an archivist by trade but a storyteller by heart. The legends passed down through generations spoke to her as tales of heroism and magic and as reflections of societal shifts and cultural tides. She wondered how these stories had morphed over centuries as they crossed lands and were told by firesides in languages her ancestors had never heard.

Across from the churchyard, old Mr. Jenkins limped towards his front gate. His movements were slow, each step a testament to years spent laboring in fields now taken over by younger hands. Eleanor watched him pause and adjust his cap—a familiar ritual—and she saw in him Merlin: wise, weathered, bearing secrets of earthy magic and ancient wisdom.

"Evening, Ellie," he called out with a nod as he noticed her on his path.

"Good evening, Mr. Jenkins," she replied with a smile. "How does your garden fare?"

"Ah," he sighed, "I suppose the earth still holds some secrets." His words hung between them like mist over morning meadows.

Back home later that evening, Eleanor sat amongst books and papers scattered across her living room floor. Each text offered different interpretations of Arthurian myths; some scholarly articles dissected Excalibur's symbolic evolution through the ages, while others delved into Merlin's portrayal across various cultural contexts. These explorations revealed how each era's preoccupations—political power struggles or quests for personal identity—shaped these stories anew.

Her cat curled up beside her on an open page about medieval chivalry. Eleanor gently lifted him off and pondered over a passage describing how knights' quests mirrored their internal battles against societal expectations and personal doubts.

The clock ticked softly in the background as she scribbled notes fervently. Her mind raced with ideas for an exhibition that would showcase these legendary artifacts and challenge visitors to see beyond the mythic to the mirrors they held up to society itself.

Could these stories still be relevant today? Could they help modern society understand its own transformations? As night deepened around her small cottage, filled with whispers from another age, Eleanor realized that perhaps what drew people continuously back to these myths was not just their quest for fantasy or escape but rather their search for meaning in times of change.

Do we not all wield our Excaliburs and seek our Merlins when faced with old and new challenges?

Unraveling the Tapestry of Myth: The Dynamic Narratives of Excalibur and Merlin

The legends of King Arthur, his mighty sword Excalibur, and the enigmatic wizard Merlin have captivated readers' imaginations for centuries. These stories are not static; they evolve with each retelling, shaped by the times and cultures they emerge from. This chapter delves into the rich tapestry of Arthurian literature, exploring how diverse textual interpretations offer a broader understanding of these legendary figures and their enduring appeal.

The Evolution of Arthurian Stories

Many authors have penned Arthurian legends across different eras, each adding their unique flavor to these age-old tales. By examining works ranging from medieval manuscripts to contemporary novels, we can trace how the characters of Excalibur and Merlin have been reshaped to meet the needs and expectations of various audiences. This exploration is not merely academic; it reveals how flexible and resilient myths can be, adapting to new generations while retaining their core essence.

Societal Influence on Myth-Making

The portrayal of Excalibur and Merlin is deeply influenced by societal shifts. As we navigate through historical contexts, from medieval times' chivalric codes to modern literature's existential queries, we see how these shifts impact storytelling. This reflection helps us appreciate not only the literary art but also gives us insight into the societal mirrors these stories provide—reflecting back the values, conflicts, and aspirations of their times.

Reflecting on Cultural Fluidity in Myths

The diversity in texts also highlights the fluid nature of myth-making. Myths are living stories, continually rewritten and reinterpreted. They serve as vessels for cultural expression and personal identification, evolving through each iteration. We open ourselves to a more nuanced understanding of past and present cultures by embracing this fluidity.

This chapter invites you to join this journey through literary landscapes shaped over centuries. It encourages a reflective engagement with texts that challenge our perceptions and broaden our horizons.

Through this exploration, we aim to foster a deeper appreciation for how cultural narratives are constructed and how they evolve—inviting us to see ourselves as part of a larger story that is always in the making.

By examining these diverse narratives, we gain insight into the artistry behind these legends and better understand the very nature of myth-making itself—how it inspires, adapts, and endures through time.

Engaging with Legends: A Personal Journey

Consider how your perceptions might shift or expand as we embark on this exploration. Reflect on what these stories—and their changes over time—might reveal about your cultural assumptions or personal values. This chapter is not just an academic exercise; it's an invitation to interact with these stories in a meaningful and transformative way.

This journey through Arthurian literature is more than just a study; it's an adventure that promises new insights and renewed inspiration from tales as old as time yet as fresh as each new interpretation we encounter. Let us move forward with curiosity and openness, ready to uncover new layers in the familiar narratives of Excalurvediveer Merlin.

In exploring the rich tapestry of Arthurian legends, one can uncover a multitude of literary interpretations that have evolved over time. These diverse narratives offer a glimpse into the ever-changing storytelling landscape, reflecting the societal and cultural influences shaping these beloved tales. **Each text brings a unique perspective, shedding light on different facets of legendary figures like Excalibur and Merlin.** By delving into these varied interpretations, readers can better understand how these stories have been reimagined and reshaped across centuries.

The evolution of Arthurian stories from medieval romances to modern retellings is a testament to their enduring appeal. Each author infuses their work with distinct themes, characterizations, and plot twists, adding complexity to the well-known myths. **By examining these diverse interpretations, readers can appreciate the nuances**

and intricacies each writer brings. Whether Tennyson's poetic rendition or Marion Zimmer Bradley's feminist take on the legends, each text offers a fresh perspective on familiar characters and events.

The evolution of Arthurian stories mirrors the ever-shifting landscape of literature, showcasing how these timeless tales continue to captivate audiences across generations. As societal values and cultural norms evolve, so do our interpretations of these legendary figures. **By immersing oneself in various literary works**, readers can trace the trajectory of Arthurian legends through different eras and genres, gaining insight into how these stories have been molded and reshaped.

Exploring textual diversity in Arthurian legends allows us to appreciate the richness and depth of these enduring tales. Each interpretation adds a new layer to the mythos surrounding King Arthur and his knights, offering fresh insights and perspectives for readers to ponder. **Engaging with various texts**, we can better understand how these stories have been reimagined to reflect changing cultural landscapes and societal values.

Embark on this journey through literary interpretations to uncover the myriad facets of Arthurian legends and witness firsthand how these timeless tales have been reshaped by different authors over time.

Exploring the various portrayals of Excalibur and Merlin in different literary works reveals that societal and cultural shifts play a significant role in shaping these interpretations. The evolution of these characters reflects the changing values, beliefs, and norms of the societies in which they were depicted. **By analyzing how Excalibur and Merlin are portrayed across different texts, readers can understand how these legends have been influenced by the contexts in which they were written.**

Excalibur, the legendary sword associated with King Arthur, has been depicted differently in various texts. It was more closely tied to divine or magical elements in earlier versions, symbolizing power and authority. However, as societal views on leadership and governance evolved, so did the portrayal of Excalibur. In some modern interpretations, Excalibur is seen as a tool for justice and equality rather than just a symbol of royal power.

Merlin, the enigmatic wizard who plays a crucial role in Arthurian legends, has also undergone transformations in different texts. His character reflects changing perceptions of magic, wisdom, and mentorship. In some stories, Merlin is portrayed as a wise and benevolent counselor to Arthur; in others, he is depicted as a more complex and morally ambiguous figure.

The diversity in portrayals of Excalibur and Merlin highlights how these legends have been adapted to resonate with contemporary audiences. As societies grapple with power, leadership, and morality issues, authors have reimagined these characters to address the concerns and values of their times. **By examining these varied interpretations**, readers can gain insights into how myths and legends are continually reshaped to reflect the cultural landscapes in which they exist.

Through the lens of different textual interpretations, readers can appreciate how Excalibur and Merlin serve as mirrors reflecting the hopes, fears, and aspirations of their respective societies. **These characters embody timeless themes such as honor, loyalty, betrayal, and redemption**, resonating with audiences across generations. **By delving into the diverse portrayals of Excalibur and Merlin**, readers can uncover layers of meaning that speak to universal truths about human nature and the complexities of our shared experiences.

As we navigate the myriad representations of Excalibur and Merlin, we are invited to consider how these legends continue to captivate our imaginations while evolving to address contemporary concerns. The enduring appeal of Arthurian tales lies in their ability to adapt to new contexts while retaining their core messages about courage, justice, and destiny. **By embracing this diversity in textual interpretations**, readers can gain a richer understanding of the Arthurian legends and the ever-changing tapestry of human storytelling.

While exploring diverse texts recounting the Arthurian legends, one can witness myth-making's ever-changing and fluid nature. The variations in storytelling styles, character portrayals, and plot developments across different literary works showcase how myths evolve and adapt over time. *By delving into these varied narratives, readers understand how myths are shaped by the societal and cultural contexts in which they are told.* Each version of the Arthurian tales reflects not only the creativity and imagination of the author but also the values, beliefs, and concerns of the era in which it was written.

The diversity found in these texts reminds us that myths are not static entities but living, breathing stories that continue to resonate with audiences through reinterpretation. Just as each retelling adds a new layer of meaning to the legends of Excalibur and Merlin, so does it contribute to the ongoing dialogue between past and present. Through this lens, readers can appreciate how myths serve as mirrors reflecting back the values and aspirations of society at different points in history.

Exploring the diversity of textual interpretations allows us to appreciate the richness and complexity of Arthurian legends. Each work offers a unique perspective on familiar characters and events, from medieval romances to modern novels. This variety enriches our understanding of the stories themselves and invites us to consider how myths can be reshaped and reimagined to suit contemporary sensibilities.

By immersing ourselves in these diverse texts, we become active participants in the myth-making process. Just as authors have reinterpreted Arthurian legends over centuries, readers can engage with these stories in ways that resonate with their own experiences. This interactive quality of myth-making highlights its dynamic nature, inviting us to question, challenge, and reinvent traditional narratives.

The fluidity of myth-making showcased in these texts underscores storytelling's power to shape our understanding of the past and present. As we navigate different versions of Arthurian legends, we realize that myths are not fixed truths but malleable narratives that reflect our ever-evolving perspectives. Embracing this fluidity allows us to appreciate these timeless tales' enduring appeal and relevance across generations.

In conclusion, by embracing textual diversity in Arthurian legends, we open ourselves to a world of infinite possibilities where myths can be reshaped, reimagined, and rediscovered. Through this exploration, we unravel the mysteries surrounding Excalibur and Merlin and embark on a journey of self-discovery where we find echoes of our own hopes, fears, and dreams within these legendary tales.

Through exploring Arthurian legends, we have ventured deep into the tapestry of texts that shape and reshape the stories of Excalibur and Merlin. By delving into diverse literary interpretations, we've seen firsthand how these narratives evolve, influenced by the societies and cultures from which they emerge. This journey broadens our understanding and enriches our appreciation for the complexity of myth-making.

The fluidity of these legends is evident as we observe how each era's values and challenges are woven into its retellings. The Arthurian tales are not static but living, breathing narratives that grow and adapt with time. This dynamic nature ensures that Excalibur and Merlin remain relevant, reflecting each generation's changing norms and ideologies.

Reflecting on the diversity of texts, we gain a more nuanced perspective of how myths serve society. They are not merely stories but powerful tools for conveying ideals, lessons, and collective hopes. As we've seen, Merlin's portrayal can shift from a wise sage to a cunning wizard, mirroring the societal pulse on authority and knowledge. Similarly, Excalibur's symbolism extends beyond a mere weapon; it represents rightful sovereignty, echoing the prevailing sentiments about leadership and justice.

This chapter underscores the value of examining multiple perspectives to grasp the full spectrum of any legend's impact. By engaging with various accounts, we witness these tales' transformation and contribute to their ongoing narrative. Each interpretation invites us to question and redefine what these stories mean to us today.

Let us carry forward this awareness that the legends of Arthur, like all myths, are mirrors reflecting human nature in its myriad forms. They challenge us to interpret, reinterpret, and ultimately understand the enduring questions of our existence more deeply. This exploration is about uncovering past truths and forging connections with our present and future.

As we move forward, let this understanding inspire us to embrace the diversity of narratives and their lessons. In doing so, we continue the timeless dialogue between past and present, between myth and reality, enriching our lives with every story we encounter.

Chapter 9: Challenging Chivalry: Revisiting Stereotypes and Historical Truths

In the dimly lit corner of the university's ancient library, Eleanor sat surrounded by towering stacks of books, each spine creased with the weight of history. Her fingers traced the delicate pages of an ancient manuscript, its edges brittle and yellowed with age. She was deep into her thesis on Arthurian legends, explicitly aiming to peel back layers of myth to reveal the gritty truths that time had shrouded.

A soft gust from an open window fluttered the pages, sending a chill down her spine—not from the cold, but from the thrill of unearthing stories untold. The air smelled of aged paper and whispers of the past. Outside, the campus lay quiet under a blanket of autumn leaves. Still, inside Eleanor's mind, a storm raged—a tempest fueled by tales of knights and wizards distorted by centuries of retellings.

She pondered over Sir Gawain, often celebrated in songs as the epitome of chivalry and honor. Yet historical accounts hinted at a more complex character shaped by political necessities rather than purely noble traits. This dissonance between legend and evidence was at the heart of her study; she sought to dismantle these glorified portrayals to reveal human flaws and political machinations inherent in their true stories.

Across from her sat Professor Hargreaves, his eyes gleaming with an enthusiasm mirroring her own. "The noble knight wasn't always so noble," he mused aloud, breaking into her thoughts. His voice echoed slightly in the quiet room. "Much like today's politicians, they played roles dictated by their society's expectations."

Eleanor nodded thoughtfully. She knew that understanding these discrepancies was essential for academic clarity and cultural insight—how modern ideals of heroism might be projections onto a past that accommodated grayer morals.

Her gaze drifted to another section in her notes about Merlin—a sage wizard archetype. Legends had painted him as an all-knowing sorcerer guiding kings with wisdom beyond mortal ken. Yet historical snippets suggested he could have been an amalgamation of earlier druidic figures and later Christian interpretations used to guide societal values through mythic influence.

As she connected these dots, Eleanor felt she was conversing with ghosts from centuries past—each one eager to correct misunderstandings wrapped around their legacy like ivy on ancient stone walls.

She looked up at Professor Hargreaves again, who smiled encouragingly before returning his focus to his ancient tome.

In this quiet pursuit nestled within crumbling pages and whispering winds through Gothic arches, did they edge closer to truths long veiled by time's tapestry? Could unraveling these threads lead us closer to understanding our history and ourselves?

Unmasking the Myth: A New Lens on Arthurian Legends

When we think of the Arthurian era, images of noble knights and wise wizards often come to mind, painting a picture that feels historic and wildly out of reach. However, these depictions are not merely innocent fabrications but are deeply rooted in centuries of storytelling that have shaped our understanding of history. This chapter seeks to peel back the layers of these enduring legends to reveal a more nuanced truth about the past.

With their chivalrous knights and magical elements, Arthurian legends have captivated audiences for centuries. Yet, beneath their romantic veneer lies a tapestry woven with historical inaccuracies and cultural misrepresentations. By dissecting these common stereotypes, we begin to see how they obscure our view of the actual people and events of the time.

The journey into Arthurian tales is often one of contradiction and adaptation. Each retelling has added layers that distance us from the original contexts of these stories. As we unpack these adaptations and inconsistencies, a different narrative emerges—one less about mythical heroes and more about the actual human conditions and societal structures that influenced these tales.

Reflecting on how modern perceptions have been shaped by such stories is crucial in understanding the past and how we view heroism and wisdom today. The image of the *noble knight* or *sage wizard* does more than entertain; it instructs and influences, often in ways we scarcely notice. It's essential to recognize how these fictional characters carry weighty expectations about virtue and intelligence that permeate our culture.

This exploration is not meant to diminish the charm or moral aspirations of Arthurian legends but to enrich our understanding by confronting what is myth and what could be historical. Such scrutiny allows us to appreciate these stories afresh, not as historical documents but as rich, evolving narratives reflecting changing societal values.

As we delve deeper into this chapter, remember that challenging long-held beliefs isn't about discarding our cultural heritage but embracing a more informed appreciation. By revisiting these stereotypes within Arthurian legends, we pave the way for a more accurate recognition of our past and, perhaps, a wiser engagement with our present.

Let's embark on this enlightening journey together, reshaping our perceptions and uncovering truths that invite us to see beyond the legend into the heart of history.

A plethora of common stereotypes have shaped our perceptions of Arthurian legends. These stereotypes often depict characters like noble knights and wise wizards in a romanticized light, blurring the lines between historical fact and fantastical fiction. **Dissecting these stereotypes and exposing the inaccuracies they perpetuate is essential to truly understand the historical truths beneath the layers of myth and legend.**

The image of the chivalrous knight, clad in shining armor and guided by a strict code of honor, has been ingrained in popular culture as the epitome of medieval virtue. However, historical evidence suggests a more nuanced reality behind this idealized archetype. **Knights were not always paragons of virtue; many were mercenaries driven by personal gain rather than lofty ideals of justice and righteousness.** By peeling back the layers of romanticism surrounding knights, we can uncover a more realistic portrait of the complexities and contradictions within medieval society.

Similarly, the figure of the sage wizard, epitomized by Merlin in Arthurian legends, often embodies wisdom, foresight, and magical prowess beyond mortal comprehension. **Yet, historical accounts paint a different picture of magic during the Arthurian period, one steeped in superstition and fear rather than grand displays of power.** By challenging the stereotype of the all-knowing wizard, we can delve into the cultural beliefs and practices that shaped perceptions of magic in ancient times.

As we unravel these common stereotypes embedded in Arthurian legends, we are confronted with a rich tapestry of historical truths waiting to be discovered. **By critically examining these stereotypes and separating fact from fiction, we can better understand the complexities and nuances present in the Arthurian era.** Through this process of exploration and analysis, we pave the way for a more authentic interpretation of history that transcends popular misconceptions.

Please continue reading to uncover how adaptations and inconsistencies further shape our understanding of Arthurian legends.

In the quest to unravel the historical truths buried beneath the layers of Arthurian legends, it becomes imperative to meticulously examine the adaptations and inconsistencies in these tales. By scrutinizing how these stories have evolved over time and across various cultures, we can create a more accurate narrative of the historical and cultural context surrounding King Arthur and his legendary court.

Adaptations, ranging from medieval manuscripts to modern-day films, have significantly shaped our perceptions of Arthurian lore. Each retelling introduces new elements, alters character dynamics, and sometimes distorts the original themes of chivalry and honor. By critically evaluating these adaptations, we can discern how societal norms and values have influenced the portrayal of Arthurian characters throughout history.

Inconsistencies within the Arthurian legends often arise due to the multiple sources from which these stories originate. Different authors, poets, and chroniclers have contributed their interpretations, resulting in plotline discrepancies, character traits, and even the portrayal of critical events. By navigating through these inconsistencies, we can identify recurring motifs and themes that persist despite variations in storytelling.

By delving into the adaptations and inconsistencies in Arthurian legends, we understand how these tales have been molded by cultural contexts and individual perspectives over centuries. This exploration allows us to reconstruct a more factual historical and cultural narrative that transcends the confines of popular stereotypes and romanticized portrayals.

Scrutinizing these adaptations enables us to discern the underlying motivations behind each retelling, shedding light on societal values prevalent at different historical points. It prompts us to question why certain aspects of the legends were emphasized or altered, revealing shifting attitudes towards heroism, loyalty, and power across diverse eras.

Navigating through inconsistencies offers us a glimpse into the complexities of oral tradition and literary transmission. It showcases how stories evolve organically over time, reflecting not only changing cultural norms but also the creative liberties of storytellers eager to leave their mark on a timeless saga.

As we embark on this journey of discovery through the adaptations and inconsistencies within Arthurian legends, we are challenged to look beyond the surface narratives and dig deeper into the historical truths waiting to be unveiled. By piecing together fragments of lore scattered across centuries, we can reconstruct a more nuanced understanding of King Arthur's realm—one that resonates with both the echoes of the past and the realities of our present day.

Reflecting on Modern Perceptions of Arthurian Characters

As we delve into the intricate web of Arthurian legends, it becomes apparent that long-standing stereotypes profoundly influence modern perceptions of characters like the noble knight and sage wizard. These stereotypes have been perpetuated through centuries of retellings, adaptations, and reinterpretations, shaping our understanding of chivalry, heroism, and magic in ways that may not align with historical truths. **It is crucial to reflect on how these preconceived notions color our view of Arthurian figures and consider how we can challenge and redefine these perceptions to unearth a more accurate representation of the past.**

The noble knight archetype, often epitomized by Sir Lancelot or Sir Gawain, embodies ideals of bravery, honor, and loyalty. However, **these portrayals have been romanticized over time**, obscuring the complexities and moral ambiguities that likely characterized individuals in the Arthurian era. By critically examining the origins of these stereotypes and how they have evolved through various cultural iterations, we can peel back the layers of myth and uncover a more nuanced understanding of medieval knighthood.

Similarly, the image of the sage wizard, most notably embodied by Merlin in Arthurian lore, conjures up notions of mysterious powers, prophetic visions, and enigmatic wisdom. **Yet, beneath this mystical facade lies a rich tapestry of historical influences**, ranging from Celtic druidic traditions to Christian symbolism. By reassessing our perceptions of wizards in medieval contexts and exploring how these characters were shaped by contemporary beliefs and fears, we can better appreciate the cultural significance they held during the Arthurian period.

The Conceptual Model in Systems Theory

The conceptual model presented in this chapter offers a unique lens through which to examine the dynamic relationship between Arthurian legends and societal norms. By visualizing these myths as interconnected systems that interact with cultural, political, and historical dimensions, **we can better appreciate how they reflect and shape broader social values**. This model highlights feedback loops where societal changes influence the evolution of legends, which subsequently impact cultural norms and perceptions.

Components of the Model

1. **Arthurian Myths**: The core component representing the body of legends surrounding King Arthur, his knights, and associated characters. These stories serve as cultural touchstones that resonate across periods.

1. **Societal Layers**: Refers to the various dimensions within a society where Arthurian myths intersect, including cultural practices, political structures, and historical events. These layers shape how the myths are interpreted and transmitted.

1. **Chivalry and Gender Roles**: Specific aspects within societal layers deeply intertwined with Arthurian narratives. Chivalry influences concepts of honor and duty among knights, while gender roles dictate women's roles in medieval societies.

Interactions within the Model

The model illustrates how changes in societal norms influence adaptations of Arthurian myths to reflect contemporary values. For example, as notions of chivalry evolved from medieval codes of conduct to Victorian ideals of gentlemanly behavior, portrayals of knights in literature adapted to suit these changing expectations.

Dynamics and Practical Implications

By understanding this model's dynamics—how societal shifts impact mythological storytelling—we gain insights into how narratives inform and are informed by cultural contexts. This awareness can guide us in critically analyzing modern retellings of Arthurian legends to discern underlying messages about societal values and norms.

In summary, by applying this conceptual model in systems theory to our exploration of Arthurian myths, we can uncover deeper truths about how these stories have shaped our perceptions of history while shedding light on contemporary societal dynamics that continue to influence our understanding of these legendary tales.

In our journey through the tapestry of Arthurian legends, we have critically examined and challenged the stereotypes that often overshadow the factual threads of history. The noble knight and the sage wizard, iconic as they are, serve not only as characters in tales but also as mirrors reflecting the values and misconceptions of different eras. By dissecting these common stereotypes, we've peeled back layers of myth to reveal a more nuanced understanding of historical truth.

The importance of this exercise cannot be overstated. We can piece together a more accurate picture of the past through questioning and revisiting the narratives handed down through generations. This task, though arduous, is essential for anyone seeking a deeper connection with history beyond the allure of legend. Each stereotype we unpacked not only showed us the inconsistencies in adaptations but also guided us in reconstructing a cultural narrative that is both informed and enlightening.

Reflecting on how modern perceptions are shaped, it becomes clear that our view of history is often colored by the lens through which we look. The stories of knights and wizards have been told countless times, each adaptation adding its hue to the palette. Understanding this helps us appreciate not just the stories themselves but also their impact on contemporary culture and our personal identities.

What we take away from this exploration is powerful: an invitation to view history with a critical eye and a curious mind. Let us carry the lessons learned here into our everyday lives, encouraging others to question, explore, and understand the past in all its complexity. By doing so, we honor the truth and enrich our collective appreciation for the stories that have shaped us.

Let this be a call to action—not just for scholars or enthusiasts but for anyone intrigued by the legends of old. Embrace this knowledge, delve deeper into the narratives you thought you knew, and discover the rich, authentic tapestries hidden beneath centuries of retelling. This pursuit of truth is an academic endeavor and a personal journey that challenges and enriches us.

As we continue this exploration in the following chapters, remember that each step taken to question and understand is a step towards a more enlightened appreciation of history and our place.

Let's move forward with the courage to ask and the eagerness to learn, unwavering in our quest for truth.

Chapter 10: Dialogue with Dragons: Engaging Culture with Historical Legends

In the dimly lit corner of a bustling café in modern-day London, Eleanor sits alone, a steaming cup of coffee forgotten beside an open book. The pages are filled with tales of Arthurian legends, the weighty themes of heroism and morality pressing on her mind like the soft hum of the city outside. She is an academic by profession, but she seeks knowledge and understanding today.

Across the room, voices merge into a gentle cacophony; laughter rings out, slicing through Eleanor's contemplation. Her eyes drift from her book to watch a young boy helping his mother navigate the crowded space. This simple act of kindness mirrors the chivalric deeds of Arthur's knights, and Eleanor wonders how these ancient ideals fit into our fast-paced, often indifferent world.

Returning to her book, she reads about Merlin's wisdom and Excalibur's might. These stories had always fascinated her as a child. Now, as she delves deeper into their cultural impact for her upcoming lecture series, she ponders their relevance in teaching contemporary values of governance and leadership.

Eleanor sips her coffee; it's cold now. She notes thoughts on how Merlin's counsel could be likened to modern-day political advisors—hidden figures shaping the course of history unseen and unsung. Could these narratives help frame new perspectives on leadership in crisis? Her pen dances across her notebook as she sketches parallels between legendary and current affairs.

Her gaze wanders again to the window where rain begins to dot the glass—a soft reminder of England's penchant for dreary weather that makes tales of knights and honor more poignant. As people rush by under umbrellas, their faces set against the storm, Eleanor reflects on how each person might carry their own Excalibur—their strength to face daily battles.

As twilight deepens and café lights grow brighter against the encroaching darkness, Eleanor packs away her notes with a sense that there is much yet to explore about these ancient tales in our modern ethos. Could understanding our past heroes give us better insight into what we value today?

ENGAGE THE PAST, TRANSFORM the Future

In this penultimate chapter, we delve into the intricate tapestry of Arthurian legends, bringing us to a critical engagement with the stories of Excalibur and Merlin. These tales are not just remnants of a distant past but vibrant narratives that continue to shape our cultural understanding of heroism, governance, and morality. By exploring these legends through a contemporary lens, we invite readers to partake in a dialogue that bridges historical insights with modern-day relevance.

The legends of King Arthur, his mighty sword Excalibur, and the enigmatic Merlin have captivated audiences for centuries. Yet, their true power lies not in their mythic splendor but in their ability to foster meaningful conversations about pivotal values and ethics today. This chapter emphasizes the necessity of dissecting these stories critically to uncover layers that can inform and inspire current and future generations.

Critical Engagement Unleashed

Our exploration begins by driving critical engagement with these narratives across various cultural settings. This approach is not merely academic but is a dynamic interaction with history and legend intertwined. By scrutinizing how different cultures interpret and integrate these legends into their societal fabric, we gain a broader understanding of their universal appeal and adaptability.

Dialogues of Relevance

Next, we initiate nuanced dialogues on the contemporary relevance of these age-old figures. What does Merlin's wisdom tell us about the leadership needed today? How does the tale of Excalibur's choosing reflect our views of justice and rightful power? These questions do not just pertain to a mythical past; they resonate deeply with ongoing discussions about leadership and moral authority in our own time.

Impact on Modern Views

Moreover, examining the impact of these dialogues on public views provides insights into how myths can shape societal norms and values. How we perceive heroism, governance, and morality through the Arthurian lens can influence real-world policies and leadership models. This reflection is crucial for understanding the potential of historical narratives to contribute to contemporary societal constructs.

Throughout this book, we have navigated through a rich landscape where myths meet reality. From uncovering the historical roots of Excalibur to demystifying Merlin's origins, each chapter has progressively built a comprehensive picture that blends legend with truth. Now, as we approach the culmination of this narrative journey, it becomes evident that understanding these myths thoroughly allows for a transformative dialogue that not only revisits history but also redefines its implications for today.

By critically engaging with these legendary narratives, readers can participate actively in cultural discourses that question and redefine ideals of leadership and morality shaped by centuries-old stories. The aim is to educate and inspire an evolved understanding that connects past lessons with present realities.

In fostering this deep connection between then and now through thoughtful reflection and dialogue, we embrace a form that might be seen as a cultural alchemy—transforming ancient narrative gold into contemporary ethical currency. Thus, as we conclude our exploration, it's clear that the legends of Excaliber and Merlin are far more than just tales of old—they are enduring conversations waiting to be engaged afresh by each new generation.

In exploring the stories of Excalibur and Merlin across different cultural settings, we uncover layers of meaning that enrich our understanding of these iconic figures. These legends transcend time and place, resonating with audiences worldwide due to their timeless themes of heroism, magic, and destiny. By delving into the various interpretations and adaptations of these tales, we gain a deeper appreciation for the enduring legacy of King Arthur and his legendary companions.

Across cultures, the figure of Merlin has been portrayed in diverse ways, reflecting the multifaceted nature of this enigmatic character. From wise counselor to powerful sorcerer, Merlin embodies the complexities of human nature and the eternal struggle between light and darkness. His presence in literature, film, and art showcases the universal fascination with wisdom and magic, sparking conversations about the role of mentors and guides in our lives.

Excalibur, the legendary sword King Arthur wields, symbolizes power, justice, and divine right. Its significance extends beyond mere weaponry to embody the ideals of chivalry and honor. Through different retellings and reinterpretations, Excalibur's symbolism evolves to mirror society's changing values and aspirations. By critically engaging with these narratives, we unearth profound insights into our collective longing for integrity and righteousness.

Cultural settings offer a rich tapestry for exploring Arthurian legends, each weaving its unique threads into the mythic fabric. Whether in medieval manuscripts or modern blockbusters, these stories captivate audiences by tapping into fundamental human desires for adventure, love, and legacy. By examining how different societies have embraced these tales, we gain a broader perspective on the enduring appeal of Arthurian lore.

The intersection of myth and reality in Arthurian legends invites us to ponder the blurred boundaries between history and storytelling. While rooted in medieval chronicles and Welsh folklore, these tales have been reshaped over centuries to suit changing tastes and ideologies. Engaging with this fluidity challenges us to question our assumptions about truth and fiction, prompting reevaluating how we perceive the past.

Dive deeper into the labyrinthine realms where history meets myth as we unravel the intricate connections between legend and cultural identity.

In exploring the contemporary relevance of Arthurian figures, it becomes evident that the legends of Excalibur and Merlin hold a timeless allure that transcends generations. These iconic characters continue to captivate audiences with their tales of bravery, magic, and wisdom, resonating with individuals across various cultural settings.

The enduring appeal of these legends lies in their ability to spark conversations about heroism, leadership, and the eternal struggle between good and evil. By initiating nuanced dialogues surrounding these figures, we can delve deeper into the moral complexities and societal reflections embedded within the stories.

ARTHURIAN LEGENDS SERVE as mirrors reflecting societal **values and aspirations,** offering a platform for introspection on contemporary issues. The character of Excalibur symbolizes power wielded with responsibility, prompting discussions on the ethical use of authority and the consequences of unchecked might. Similarly, Merlin's wisdom and foresight invite contemplation on the role of guidance and mentorship in navigating today's complex world. **Engaging with these figures encourages individuals to ponder their values and beliefs**, fostering a deeper understanding of personal ethics and societal responsibilities.

Through dialogue and reflection on Arthurian legends, individuals can uncover universal truths that resonate across cultures. The themes of loyalty, sacrifice, and redemption woven into these stories provide insights into human nature and the complexities of relationships. By exploring the motivations and dilemmas faced by characters like King Arthur or Morgana le Fay, readers can draw parallels to their own experiences, gaining valuable perspectives on loyalty, betrayal, and forgiveness.

The contemporary relevance of Arthurian figures extends beyond literature and folklore, influencing modern interpretations of leadership, morality, and justice. By critically engaging with these legends in various cultural contexts, individuals can gain a deeper appreciation for the nuances of character development and narrative complexity in the stories. **These dialogues open doors to exploring themes of legacy, destiny, and the cyclical nature of history**, prompting reflections on how past narratives shape present identities.

In today's rapidly changing world, the lessons embedded in Arthurian legends offer timeless wisdom that transcends temporal boundaries. By initiating nuanced dialogues on the contemporary relevance of Excalibur and Merlin, individuals can glean valuable insights into personal growth, moral decision-making, and societal change. **These conversations pave the way for a deeper understanding of human nature**, inspiring individuals to reflect on their roles in shaping a more just and compassionate world.

Engaging with the myths surrounding Excalibur and Merlin in diverse cultural settings can help individuals uncover layers of meaning that resonate deeply with their own experiences. **By delving into these narratives with an open mind and a critical eye**, readers can learn about courage, integrity, and the enduring quest for truth. **The contemporary relevance of Arthurian figures lies in their historical significance and their ability to inspire meaningful conversations about identity, purpose, and the eternal struggle between light and darkness.**

As we navigate these dialogues on Arthurian legends' contemporary relevance, we are reminded of our shared humanity and interconnectedness across time and space. **The stories of Excalibur and Merlin serve as guiding beacons**, illuminating paths toward self-discovery, empathy, and collective growth. Through thoughtful reflection and open-minded discourse, we can continue unraveling the mysteries enshrined within these legendary tales, drawing inspiration from their enduring wisdom to navigate our journeys with courage and grace.

In engaging with the cultural significance of Arthurian legends, we uncover a profound impact on public perceptions of heroism, governance, and morality. Through thoughtful dialogue and critical analysis of iconic figures like Excalibur and Merlin, we begin to unravel the intricate threads that weave through our societal understanding of these concepts. **By examining the tales of Excalibur and Merlin with a discerning eye, we open doors to more profound reflections on what it means to be heroic, how governance shapes our societies, and the moral compass by which we navigate our lives.**

Heroism, often portrayed in grand gestures and epic battles in Arthurian legends, takes on new dimensions when dissected through the lens of critical engagement. We realize that heroism is not merely about physical prowess or noble lineage but encompasses virtues like courage, sacrifice, and compassion. **By delving into the stories of**

Excalibur and Merlin, we are prompted to question our definitions of heroism and consider how we can embody these qualities in our everyday lives.

Governance, a central theme in Arthurian tales, with the legendary sword symbolizing rightful rule, invites us to reflect on the nature of leadership and power. Exploring the narratives surrounding Excalibur confronts notions of just governance, accountability, and the responsibilities that come with authority. **This dialogue prompts us to evaluate our current governance systems. It inspires us to strive for leadership, prioritizing justice, equality, and the common good.**

Morality, intricately woven into the fabric of Arthurian legends through characters like Merlin, who navigate complex ethical dilemmas, compels us to ponder our ethical frameworks. As we engage with these stories, we confront moral quandaries, ethical choices, and the consequences of our actions. **Through this exploration, we are challenged to reassess our moral compass, cultivate virtues such as integrity and wisdom, and strive toward a more ethical way of being in the world.**

The impact of engaging with these dialogues is transformative, shaping not only our individual perspectives but also influencing broader societal views on heroism, governance, and morality. As we grapple with the complexities presented in Arthurian legends, we are called to introspection, dialogue with others, and action toward creating a more just and virtuous society. **Ultimately, these reflections inspire us to embody the values inherent in these timeless tales – courage in adversity, wisdom in leadership, and integrity in moral choices – as we navigate the complexities of our modern world.**

As we delve into the heart of **Arthurian legends**, we uncover tales of heroism and magic and insights into the fabric of cultural discourse. Through the lens of critical engagement, this chapter has illuminated how **Excalibur and Merlin** are more than mere characters of folklore;

they are pivotal in shaping conversations around governance, morality, and heroism in today's society.

Step 1: Driving Critical Engagement with Excalibur and Merlin

Engaging with these stories across diverse cultural settings has revealed their universal appeal and adaptability. By exploring how different cultures interpret these legends, we foster a global appreciation of their relevance, encouraging a rich tapestry of perspectives that resonate in modern times.

Step 2: Initiating Nuanced Dialogues on Contemporary Relevance

The initiation of nuanced dialogues helps bridge the ancient past with the present, inviting us to reflect on contemporary issues through the prism of Arthurian values. Such discussions enrich our understanding and challenge us to reconsider modern ideals of leadership and ethics.

Step 3: Analyzing the Impact of Dialogues on Public Views

Evaluating the impact of these dialogues on public perceptions has been enlightening. By understanding how these narratives influence today's views on leadership and morality, we gain insights into the power of storytelling in shaping societal values and inspiring positive change.

Step 4: Encouraging Continued Engagement and Exploration

Lastly, encouraging ongoing engagement with these stories ensures that the wisdom of the past continues to inform the future. By providing resources for further exploration, we invite readers to keep the dialogue alive, perpetuating a cycle of learning and reinterpretation that keeps these legends vibrant and relevant.

This process deepens our understanding of Excalibur and Merlin and enhances our grasp of their historical roots and mythological constructs. From here, readers are equipped to discern fact from fiction, appreciating both these tales' mythical allure and historical significance.

As we conclude our exploration with **"The Sword and the Sage,"** it is clear that the true power of these legends lies in their ability to adapt and resonate across ages. By engaging critically with these stories, we preserve their legacy and enrich our cultural dialogue, ensuring that the lessons of the past continue to illuminate the paths of the future. Let us carry forward this enriched understanding, embracing the complexities of these narratives as guides in our quest for wisdom and insight.

Epilogue

Embracing the Legends, Unveiling the Truths
As we draw the curtain on our journey through the misty realms of Excalibur and Merlin, we come away enriched with knowledge that does more than satisfy our curiosity—it empowers us. The stories of old are not just tales to be told; they are beacons guiding us through the complexities of history and myth, illuminating paths of understanding and personal relevance.

In this exploration, we've unraveled the tapestry of legends to reveal the threads of truth hidden within. From the historical origins of the Arthurian legends to the symbolic meanings behind Merlin's wisdom and Excalibur's might, we've journeyed together through a landscape rich in narrative and meaning. I hope these insights have not only informed but also inspired—encouraging a deeper appreciation for how our past informs our present.

The insights gleaned here are tools—much like Excalibur—meant to be wielded in your personal and professional quests. Whether you're a historian, educator, or enthusiast, understanding these legends can enhance your perspective in discussions and writings or enrich your storytelling.

Reflecting on Our Journey

We've dissected myths to uncover their factual cores, navigating centuries-old misconceptions to a clearer view of history's truths. This process is invaluable not only for academic purposes but also for personal growth. Understanding the distinction between myth and fact sharpens critical thinking skills, enabling us to approach modern myths discerningly.

For those inspired by Merlin's wisdom or stirred by the power of Excalibur, consider how these elements can be metaphorically applied to overcome challenges or lead with integrity in your own life. The sage's wisdom teaches us about insight and foresight—qualities essential for personal development and leadership.

Toward Further Horizons

While we've covered extensive ground, no single volume can capture all facets of such rich traditions. Areas ripe for further exploration include deeper archaeological investigations into early British history or a more detailed comparative analysis between different versions of Arthurian tales across cultures.

I encourage you to continue this quest for knowledge. Dive into primary historical documents, seek out academic discussions, or craft your own interpretations of these stories through creative expressions.

A Call to Action

Let the stories of Merlin and Excalibur inspire you not merely as tales from the past but as enduring lessons in courage, leadership, and wisdom. Embrace these narratives in your life's endeavors; let them guide your decisions and enrich your understanding of the world's vast tapestries.

As you turn this page in our shared adventure, carry the torch of inquiry and insight. Let it illuminate your path as you forge ahead into new territories of knowledge and understanding.

"Legends are lessons; they ring with truths." - Neil Gaiman

May this book serve as both a map and compass in your ongoing quest for truth amid the shadows cast by myth?

References

(1999). U.S. Immigration Policy and the Plight of Its Unskilled Workers. https://core.ac.uk/download/5132952.pdf

Powerful Christian Testimonies (2024). https://thewitness.org/powerful-christian-testimonies/

Overpowered Sword Manga - Decore of Home. https://decoreofhome.com/2024/01/27/overpowered-sword-manga/

Watercolor Dreams - Adding Artistic Flair to Your Photo Edits - Rhodes Caribbean. http://rhodes-caribbean.com/business/watercolor-dreams-adding-artistic-flair-to-your-photo-edits.htm

Optimize Payload Airlift Airbags for Trucks - All Air Springs. https://www.allairsprings.com/optimize-payload-airlift-airbags-for-trucks/

Tag: secret of Dante's realm · kevinhq.com. https://kevinhq.com/tags/secret-of-dantes-realm/

Schaar, E. (2015). Peter Coffin. Artforum International., 54(2), 332.

Yoga teacher training in India | Shree Hari Yoga School. https://shreehariyoga.com/samadhipada-limbs-of-yoga-defined/

Writing Prompts about A Rose for Emily - Essay Ideas, Research Questions, & More. https://assignzen.com/writing-prompts/a-rose-for-emily-essay-ideas/

Rapunzel. https://www.shinfieldplayers.org.uk/show-reviews/rapunzel

Liu, S. Y. (2016). The Jewel for the Crown: Reconsidering Female Kingship and Queenship in the Galfridian Historiography. Palgrave Macmillan US EBooks. https://doi.org/10.1057/978-1-137-58381-9_4

Lowans, C., & Foley, A. (2024). Sustainable Development in Third Level Programs: Distilling a Pathway to a True Net-Zero Education. Sustainability, 16(5), 1998.

. Search Engines that Learn from Their Users. https://doi.org/10.1145/2964797.2964817

Unearthing Boston's Hidden Treasures: A Fascinating Metal Detecting Journey - detection.com. https://detection.com/unearthing-bostons-hidden-treasures-a-fascinating-metal-detecting-journey/

Chapter Chapter 2 | The Long Way Down by TheWritingReaper at Inkitt. https://www.inkitt.com/stories/horror/271172/chapters/2

Airplane Flying Backwards Dream Meaning: What Does It Symbolize?. https://insidemydream.com/airplane-flying-backwards-dream-meaning/

Impermanence is a way of life in the earthly realm | Moovly gallery. https://www.moovly.com/gallery/video/impermanence-is-a-way-of-life-in-the-earthly-realm/c1878d35-0f74-4d21-9b4f-34d7cb43d251

Five Laboratory Changes in Rheumatology - Rheumatologist OnCall - Inflammatory Arthritis Diagnosis & Treatment. https://rheumatologistoncall.com/2021/05/22/laboratory-changes-in-rheumatology/

Unlock Limitless Thrills at SM Togel: A Comprehensive Guide to Dominating Online Gaming and Winning Big – Uvwbql. https://uvwbql.com/unlock-limitless-thrills-at-sm-togel-a-comprehensive-guide-to-dominating-online-gaming-and-winning-big/

Tag: Dietary Habits Karma Health Hub. https://karma-laboratory.com/tag/dietary-habits/

Our Blog – 911papers. https://911papers.com/our-blog/

Garmon, L. (1981). Shilly-Shally Solutions. Science News. https://doi.org/10.2307/3966314

The Mind Behind Amazon: Unveiling Jeff Bezos's Psychological Profile - The Brain Blog. https://thebrain.blog/jeff-bezoss-psychological-profile/

Python Programming Training Online Course I Skill Developers. https://skilldevelopers.com/event/introduction-to-python/

Maximizing Home Improvement Leads with Social Media Marketing. https://www.rrmathome.com/blogs/maximizing-home-improvement-leads-with-social-media-marketing/

FFS Orientations at TCNE First Event — Facialteam. https://facialteam.eu/blog/ffs-orientations-at-tcne-first-event-in-january/

The Power of Sparring Video Review: Unlocking Your Martial Arts Potential. https://www.dfmcoaching.com/post/the-power-of-sparring-video-review-unlocking-your-martial-arts-potential

Unveiling the Mystery: How Long Did Buddha Meditate?. https://vitalflowing.com/unveiling-the-mystery-how-long-did-buddha-meditate

SGE Explorer Stickers set #3 • Spartan & the Green Egg. https://www.spartanandthegreenegg.com/product/sge-explorer-stickers-set-3/?add-to-cart=4069

Famous Love Problem Solution In Nottingham - Famous Free Astrologer In india. http://www.mohamedabdullahkhadhim.in/famous-love-problem-solution-in-nottingham/

Understanding education research through PDFs: A comprehensive guide. https://mmcalumni.ca/blog/understanding-the-importance-and-impact-of-education-research-pdf-a-comprehensive-overview

STP Platform Networking (January 2024) | Digital Service Hub. https://sp.hkstp.org/events-and-happenings/platform-networking-january-2024

Romeo And Juliet - foodspie.com. https://foodspie.com/romeo-and-juliet/

Dullahan: Mythical Headless Horseman of Irish Folklore - IrishWishes. https://irishwishes.com/dullahan/

(2015). History and the Making and Remaking of Wales. https://doi.org/10.1111/1468-229X.12141

Free FapHouse Vintage Premium Account and Password — [Updated July, 2024]. https://www.passworrrds.com/free-faphouse-vintage-premium-account-password/

Peony: An Everlasting Muse in Art and Culture | Artificial Flowers Suppliers. http://www.artificial-flowers-suppliers.com/peony-an-everlasting-muse-in-art-and-culture/

Exploring the Beauty of Natural Things: Names, Significance, and Conservation. https://gov-byx-j.top/2023/11/13/exploring-the-beauty-of-natural-things-names-significance-and-conservation/

Pedagogies of Translation: Lecture and Workshop Series | Barnard Center for Engaged Pedagogy. https://cep.barnard.edu/pedagogies-translation-lecture-and-workshop-series

Shield Security Plugin Update: Addressing CVE-2023-6989 -. https://www.im4rent.com/2024/02/13/shield-security-plugin-update-addressing-cve-2023-6989/

Unveiling The Enchantment Purple Days Fanfic Explained. https://buzzmuzz.com/purple-days-fanfic/

Ironic Movie Quotes – The Daily Quip. https://thedailyquip.com/movie-quotes/ironic-movie-quotes/

How Celine Hoodie T Shirt Redefines Style | Shoot Bloging. https://www.shootbloging.com/how-celine-hoodie-t-shirt-redefines-style/

Wright, M. K. (2023). Hulihia Nā Kānāwai ʻĀina: The Effects of Post-1893 Land Law Changes On Native Hawaiians - Population Demographics Supplement or Supplant? https://core.ac.uk/download/590218006.pdf

Something or Nothing: Freedom and Negativity in Beckett and Adorno — Royal Holloway Research Portal. https://pure.royalholloway.ac.uk/en/publications/something-or-nothing-freedom-and-negativity-in-beckett-and-adorno

Lester, A. (2014). Homing in: Alfred Russel Wallace's homes in Britain (1852 to 1913). http://wallacefund.info/sites/wallacefund.info/files/Lester.2014.The_Linnean%2C_30%282%29.22-32.pdf

Keep Improving Along the Way – Showcase Magazine. https://showcasemagazine.com/2024/02/01/keep-improving-along-the-way/

Medusa - Edu Press Publishers. https://edupresspublishers.com/2024/02/06/medusa/

Tollywood Superstar Dev Embarks on a Thrilling Journey as Feluda in Upcoming Bengali Cinema Adaptation ? | Cinekolkata.com. https://cinekolkata.com/

tollywood/tollywood-superstar-dev-embarks-on-a-thrilling-journey-as-feluda-in-upcoming-bengali-cinema-adaptation/

Watch Video from Collaboration Between The Wheel's Leadership Academy and iCommunity - iCommunity. https://www.icommunityhub.org/watch-video-from-collaboration-between-the-wheels-leadership-academy-and-icommunity/

Etched In Stone. https://www.thetableqc.com/post/2017/07/05/etched-in-stone

Don't miss out!

Visit the website below and you can sign up to receive emails whenever Myrddin Sage publishes a new book. There's no charge and no obligation.

https://books2read.com/r/B-A-JBAOB-PTCQD

BOOKS 2 READ

Connecting independent readers to independent writers.

Also by Myrddin Sage

Mythic Japan: Unlocking the Legends of Gods and Heroes
Echoes of Enchantment: Navigating the Magic of Celtic Mythology
Echoes of Valhalla: Unveiling the Modern Wisdom of Norse Myths
Gods Among Us: The Power and Intrigue of Roman Mythology
The Sword and the Sage: Unveiling the Truth of Excalibur and Merlin

About the Author

At 67, Myrddin Sage steps into the spotlight as a newly published author, bringing a tapestry of rich life experiences and a vibrant imagination. His journey from a Navy Veteran to a Retired Dispatcher of Messengers has endowed him with profound insights into human cultures and the natural world. As Myrddin introduces his debut novel, he shares a narrative infused with wisdom, whimsy, and a deep respect for the interconnectedness of life. Drawing on his academic background and extensive travels, Myrddin's work explores themes of adventure, discovery, and the transformative power of knowledge. With his first publication, he proves that new chapters can be embarked upon at any stage of life, inspiring readers with the message that it is always the right time to follow one's passions.

www.ingramcontent.com/pod-product-compliance
Lightning Source LLC
Chambersburg PA
CBHW020601160726
47991CB00002B/819